Oliver Perry Fradenburgh

Twenty-five Stepping Stones toward Christ's Kingdom

Oliver Perry Fradenburgh

Twenty-five stepping Stones toward Christ's Kingdom

ISBN/EAN: 9783337183936

Printed in Europe, USA, Canada, Australia, Japan

Cover: Foto ©Lupo / pixelio.de

More available books at **www.hansebooks.com**

TWENTY-FIVE

STEPPING STONES

TOWARD

CHRIST'S KINGDOM.

BY

O. P. FRADENBURGH,

LIBERTY, N. Y.

CONTENTS.

FIRST STEP.
Man 7

SECOND STEP.
The Holy Spirit 14

THIRD STEP.
Holy Men of Old.. 22

FOURTH STEP.
Imputed Righteousness Answered...................... 33

FIFTH STEP.
Think 43

SIXTH STEP.
Final Perseverance of the Saints and Bible Twisting...... 43

SEVENTH STEP.
The Kingdom of God.................................... 61

EIGHTH STEP.
Ante-Christ 69

NINTH STEP.
The Two Witnesses..................................... 79

TENTH STEP.
Baptism and Hobby-Horses.............................. 91

ELEVENTH STEP.
Communion and Eating Christ........................... 99

TWELFTH STEP.
The Sabbath vs. The Lord's Day........................ 104

THIRTEENTH STEP.
Eating and Drinking 111

FOURTEENTH STEP.
Ye Are Gods.. 118

FIFTEENTH STEP.
Is the End of the Age and the Coming of the Lord Near?... 125

SIXTEENTH STEP.
Fools 130

SEVENTEENTH STEP.
The Church of Rome.................................... 138

EIGHTEENTH STEP.
War 144

NINETEENTH STEP.
Christ in Politics...................................... 151

TWENTIETH STEP.
Money and Religion..................................... 154

TWENTY-FIRST STEP.
Christian Perfection 159

TWENTY-SECOND STEP.
Good Will to Men....................................... 167

TWENTY-THIRD STEP.
Martin Luther 174

TWENTY-FOURTH STEP.
Adam's Fall 184

TWENTY-FIFTH STEP.
Virginity 193

TWENTY-SIXTH STEP.
The Fish Story... 196

TWENTY-SEVENTH STEP.
Free Methodist Perfection..... 200

PREFACE.

You will find that the Twenty-five Stepping Stones are firmly founded on the Rock, so you can stand upon them with safety, for the great truths they contain I received by direct revelation, through the Spirit, and on January 16th, 1891, God sent his angel to anoint me to restore to the church the faith and teachings of the Apostolic Church, or in other words, to be one of the witnesses of Revelations XI. This you will not believe, for no prophet is honored in his own country. But if you will send to Scribner's Sons $20 you can get ten volumes of the writings of the Ante-Nicene Fathers, and they will prove to you that I teach nothing but what was taught in the Apostolic Church. (My set cost nearly twice as much). In short I will recant any doctrine that I hold that they did not teach, for they taught the whole council of God. If I am not the Elijah that was for to come and restore all things, I have usurped his place and am doing his work, and it is for you to say whose work I am doing. (Read 9th Step.) The full account of my experience and unjust imprisonment is told in a book of 30 large pages, entitled. "Twice Kidnapped;" price 15 cents. The Stepping Stones lead to the door of the Kingdom. When you have stepped on them all you will want the keys to get in, so send 50 cents for "Saint Peter's Keys, or The Mystery of Christ's Kingdom Revealed," and you will get a book of about 100 large pages, equal to 125 of these, that will tell the whole story. This book has proved a blessing to many and many have rejoiced to get it. The most eminent and best learned Christian physician here says: "Next to the Bible it it the most important book published." I did not get the truth from the "Fathers," for I received it by direct revelation before I saw or heard of them, but I have quoted from them largely, thinking you would accept truth from them rather than from me, and two witnesses are better than one. Praying that a blessing will follow your reading this book, I remain yours for the Kingdom,

O. P. FRADENBURGH,

Liberty, N. Y.

September 20th, 1900.

FIRST STEP.

Man.

In the first chapter in the Bible you will find my text; also in the last. In short you can hardly open the Bible without finding it, as it occurs many thousand times. Yet, perhaps no word in our language is so difficult to define. A college professor in trying to define it to his class called man an unfeathered biped. One of his students plucked or unfeathered a hen, presented it, exclaiming: "Behold your man!"

One morning as Israel was emerging from their tents they saw the ground covered with a white substance. They looked at it and said man-na, which means: What is it? They touched it and said man-na, and tasted it and repeated man-na, and it was man-na. When we see a being created in the image of God go staggering through the street or lying in the gutter, we say manna, for no word will define him. To call him a brute would slander the brute. Was that the crowning work of God's glorious creation over which the morning stars sang together and the sons of God shouted for joy? Yet he has a better right to a name than he whose greed for gain is responsible for his being in that condition. Of him also we say, manna.

Of those who come to Christ making strong claims of friendship and service, He replies, "I never knew you." "What is man that thou art mindful of him? and the son of man that thou visitest him?" says the Psalmist. A man promotes one who has long served him in a less responsible position and gives him the keys of his wealth, but he betrays his trust and absconds with his benefactor's wealth, who replies with bitterness, "I never knew you, but I vainly thought I did." He finds the truth of this. The heart is deceitful above all things and desperately wicked. Who can know it?

In South Africa we find a powerful and so called Christian nation has pounced on two little Christian republics like a wolf on a couple of kids, to rob them of their lives, liberties and homes, and all to satisfy their greed for gold. Is England willing to barter her soul for those gold and diamond mines. Is not Christ answering them to-day, "I never knew you." God well says, "Behold, the nations are as a drop in bucket, and are counted as the small dust of the balance. Behold, He taketh up the isles as a very little thing, and Lebanon is not suffered to burn, or the beasts thereof for a burnt offering. All the nations are as nothing before Him; they are counted to Him less than nothing, and vanity."

God created the horse, cow, sheep, dog, poultry, and other useful animals to serve man, and surely no man could devise more faithful servants. They take pride in obeying their master, which appears to be the instinct of their own nature. But for what purpose was man created? Was it to serve God? If so, He made a great blunder and the infallible failed, for the mind of the flesh is enmity against God, for it is not subject to the law of God, neither, indeed, can it be; and they that are in the flesh cannot please God. So you see he is neither a friend nor a servant. Yet the Word says: "Thou hast made him but little lower than God and crowneth him with glory and honor." Yet where is the glory and honor?

The time has come to solve the mystery of man that has perplexed the ages. Although all modern efforts to live in perfect subjection to God's law have failed, although many have professed to, but they have made a sorry lead of it, and the greatest theologians deny that is is possible to live without sinning against God. Spurgeon was asked his opinion of the sinless people. He replied: "I do not think much of them. I employed some to work in my garden; they come late and quit early; spent most of their night at their meetings, and the weeds thrived better than the vegetables under their care; so I discharged them and hired sinners in their place, with better results." While we admit that Spurgeon was a great and successful preacher, we would not take a man that used tobacco and died with the gout, for a model.

To get at man's trouble we have got to go back to creation and Eden, for we cannot successfully prescribe for a disease until we find its origin, cause and nature, and that has been the trouble with modern theologians; they have been trying to treat sin without knowing what it was. God never made a mistake, and when he created Adam he placed him in honor next to himself and above all the angels, and only capable of committing but one sin, and that he could have easily refrained from, for God gave him but one command, and that was not to eat of the tree; but God knew he would, and knew the serpent would tempt him. If Adam had not fallen man never could have earned his future reward, for it would be their nature to love and obey God as it is the horse or dog to obey their master, so they carry out the instinct of their nature and do not earn a future reward. Adam's sin entirely reversed man's nature, so the things that he most desires to do are the most heinous in God's sight, and the things that God would have him do are the most displeasing to him. It is true in nature that when a man makes a personal sacrifice to please or benefit another he earns a reward, but not when he lives for his own pleasures only. So when we abandon the pleasures of this life we earn a future reward. When Adam by breaking a single law fell from the great honor and glory in which he was placed and dragged down his seed with him to be instead of a son of God a nameless what is it, God intended that thousands of years should elapse before any one should find the way back to God's favor and sonship, and then only by great trials and suffering.

As soon as man fell God commenced the work of his restitution by teaching him to offer burnt sacrifices, which was a type of the great sacrifice that was to follow. Do not deceive yourself by thinking that these offerings typify Christ's sufferings only, yet that has been the stumbling stone over which the church has fallen for 1500 years, while the Bible nowhere teaches it. I do not mean the cross, but its true meaning. If man had not fallen Christ and his elect could never have had a kingdom for want of subjects. All who obeyed the law of burnt offerings and all who lived before Christ that will be saved, will be resurrected and placed on the renewed earth where Christ and his saints will reign over them during the millenium, at the end of which they will be subjected to a great tribulation, in which a few will be washed white but the great majority will fall and be lost. This applies equally to members of the popular church of to-day. But God has far better things for those of us who wish, and will pay the price.

There are three steps leading to the Kingdom. First, conversion, which is turning from our evil ways and receiving pardon for past sins; but this does not change our nature nor desire for sin, nor lessen Satan's power over us, but is what all professors have or should receive. This is as far as Paul got when he wrote, "When I would do good evil is present with me," and, "the things I hate, them I do." But he had reached another experience when he wrote, "Now I rejoice in my sufferings for your sake and fill up on my part that which is lacking of the afflictions of Christ in my flesh for his body's sake, which is the church." Enduring this affliction enabled him to say, "No longer I live but Christ liveth in me." How he got this experience ought to greatly interest us all. First by receiving the Holy Spirit, which all are permitted to receive if they earnestly seek Him, and He will convict us of all sin and lead us into all truth and show us what sacrifice will be pleasing to God. The Spirit does not make us perfect as some teach, but shows us what is between us and Christ and how to remove it and strengthens us to all endurance. The third and final step is to be whipped into the kingdom or sonship, for we will not go in without, for whom the Lord loveth he chasteneth, and scourgeth every son whom he receiveth. If we are without chastening whereof all sons are partakers, then are we bastards and not sons. Is the modern church producing bastards or sons?

A lady took to her home a homeless orphan. She said, I must try and prove his honesty. So she took him to his room and said, "You may have that old bureau to put your clothes in, and the old trumpery in it you may put in this box, it has not been in use for years." She had put a quarter of a dollar among its contents, and when she left him to clean it out she left the door ajar and quietly came back to see what came of the quarter. When he found it he put it in his pocket, saying, "Surely it has been here for years and no one knows of it," but on second thought, he said, "Surely this is not mine and it doubtless belongs to the good lady that so kindly gave me a home, and shall I repay her by robbing her!" So he took it from his pocket and put it on the bureau and knelt down and prayed God to forgive the thought of his heart and to give strength to resist temptation. The next moment he was in her arms, and said, "My dear boy, I fear I have tried you too severely, and fear my own sons would not have resisted as well. You are no longer my servant, but I will make you my son, and you shall share equally with my own sons." That is just the way the Lord tries us who shall sit as a refiner and purifier of silver, and he shall purify the sons of Levi and purge them as gold and silver; but who may abide the day of his coming.

Conversion, as I said, removes love for sin without removing temptation or desire for it, while this scourging frees us from Satan's power and makes all sin so heinous that it is impassable, because it destroys original sin and makes us like Adam before the fall, only to repeat his sin will be beyond our power. To illustrate, one man drinks whiskey and becomes intoxicated, another does not like whiskey but drinks lager, with the same result; another ale, another wine, another brandy, and another cider, and all with the same result. While they are all different the alcohol, the intoxicating property, is the same in all. Remove that and they could drink any or all without effect. But remove the alcohol and the drinkers would soon lose their appetite for them. What alcohol is to these drinks, original sin is to the sins of the world. Remove that and you will find that you are dead to the world but alive to God, and you can say with Paul, "No longer I live but Christ liveth in me." That is what Christ meant when he said, "Ye must be born again."

When I attended the district school in the little "tadpole" schoolhouse, part of my work was to solve arithmetical problems or "do sums," as we called it, some of which had several answers. It was not sufficient to get one or two of them right, but all of them must correspond with the answers in the book or the teacher would say your work is all wrong, rub it out and begin again. So it is in solving the great problem of sin and salvation. The Bible is our text book and the Holy Spirit is our teacher, and when we get a faith that takes in the whole Bible we will know that we have got the correct solution. If we say we are tempted to sin or do evil we have not got this answer. We know that whosoever is born of God sinneth not, but he that is begotten of God keepeth himself and the wicked one toucheth him not. He that committeth sin is of the devil. Whosoever is born of God doth not commit sin, for his seed remaineth in him and he cannot sin because he is born of God. We are then admitted in the great family of God. Christ said, "He that sinneth is the servant of sin, and the servant abideth not in the house forever, but the son abideth forever." When we have received the divine nature it will be as impossible for us to sin as it is for God. You cannot expect me to explain all in this First Step, but if you follow me I will endeavor to make all plain. It was not enough for me to get the required answer, but I had to tell how I got it and to give a reason for working it so. So we must give a reason for the hope that is in us, as how we are saved by Christ's death, and why God could not save the world without the sacrifice of his son.

SECOND STEP.

The Holy Spirit.

"Be not drunken with wine wherein is excess, but be ye filled with the Spirit."—Eph. 5:18. "If you have not the Spirit of Christ you are none of his."

For four thousand years salvation was obtainable to those who sought it without the aid of the Holy Spirit, or before He was given to the world, and it is as much so now, and His power and presence is but little felt in most churches to-day, yet they imagine they are guided and taught by Him, as they think all receive Him at the time of conversion, and I see the revisers of the New Testament have changed "Have you received the Holy Ghost since you believed" to "Did you receive the Holy Ghost when you believed," in Acts 19: 2. If all did why did Paul ask the question? And the answer proves an exception to the rule, if it is the rule. Also, the Samaritans did not receive Him at the time of their conversion and baptism, Acts, 8: 14-17. Neither did Paul receive Him at the time and place of his conversion. Dr. Garden says He is received subsequently to and independent from the time and action of conversion.

He shall convict the world of sin. When a minister enters his pulpit filled with the Spirit, He, the Spirit, exerts an irresistible power over the sinners of his congregation that causes them to cry out in agony and seek the Lord many times before an invitation is given. It was that Spirit that caused an audience to cling to the back of their seats when a filled preacher was preaching on sliding into hell.

It was the cause of Moody's success of ten years ago, and is the only true source of success one can have, for the Spirit is the only convicting power in the world, yet many conduct what they call successful revivals who have never received Him. They can convince men by argument that it is their duty to be converted and join the church. They will say hold up your hand if you want us to pray for you. I guess you are all right now, so come and join our church; while they have never been convicted nor converted. Our churches are too full of such members to-day. I heard a minister say in a sermon, "I have got over 100 members, but would rather have ten good working members than to have the whole of you." Another said, "If the devil came and took half of you I would not dare to say: Stop, devil! For I would not know as he was taking more than belonged to him." The members are not alone to blame, for a minister recently in speaking of business matters, said: "It has got so that no one is to be trusted." I told him the old adage, "Like priest, like people," holds good, for I had sent or handed my book to over 500 ministers, with a request to give their opinion, and if they could prove me wrong in any part to let me know. Many promised to do so when they took it, but I have their united approval, if silence gives consent, for I have enough of that to fill volumes. I got one response, and he said a certain passage should be taken spiritually, but failed to tell me how, and did not give his address, so I could answer. To spiritualize the literal teaching of Christ is taking the Spirit with a vengeance, or a polite way for saying we do not believe it. Paul's prophecy to Timothy, 4: 3, "For the time will come when they will not endure sound doctrine, but after their own lust shall they heap to themselves teachers having itching ears, and they shall turn away their ears from the truth and shall be turned unto fables." That means they will have teachers whose ears will itch to know what will be best pleasing to their hearers and not what is most profitable.

"Be not drunken with wine wherein is excess, but be ye filled with the Spirit." The power of the Spirit is compared to intoxication in its appearance, so those who first saw His effect supposed them to be drunken and Peter had to explain. I am sorry to say that not many such explanations are necessary in these days. Occasionally we hear of some who are prostrated by His power, while modest professors ridicule. It is not only necessary to be filled, but remain full. Many press forward and obtain Him and receive some of His gifts, so sinners fall before them, as in Moody's past experience, or the sick are raised by their magic touch, but it did not last very long, for the road He marked out was too rugged and the cross too burdensome and something was asked that would not be popular for them to teach, and so the Kingdom is never reached. The spiritual wilderness between Egypt and the Jordan is as thickly strewed with the carcasses of the fallen as the literal one was. We must first stop to count the cost, for if there is anything on earth that we prize above Christ's Kingdom we had not better start, for it will surely be required, for He said: "Unless a man forsaketh all that he hath he cannot be my disciple."

Our religion is not a mechanical religion that one can work himself in by outward acts only, but a spiritual religion. The access to the Kingdom can only be obtained by the aid of the Holy Spirit, yet we can obtain a salvation by service without Him but not a crown. His office is to take possession of our temples and by teaching assist us by stimulating us to endure all necessary cleansing to prepare it for the abode of the Son of God. Many hold that we are perfect as soon as we receive the Comforter, but this is not so, any more than it is true a student is graduated as soon as he enters college. The Spirit's work can be illustrated best by the telephone wire stretched from us to God and through Him we send and receive messages. "He takes the things of God and shows them unto us," but as we cannot telephone without the connecting wire, neither can we approach to Christ without the Spirit. He will teach all who will listen to and obey His voice. When He tells us to do or not do a thing and we refuse He will talk to us no more, but leave us.

As to what method the Spirit uses in teaching us is a subject on which theologians differ. Some hold that the Spirit only uses the Word, or Bible, to teach with, while those that hold that faith have divided the church into 1000 different sects, all of which differ in some points of doctrine. I heard D. L. Moody teach that in a sermon preached in the great Brooklyn revival of 1894, and said he had no faith in them who claim to have dreams and visions; while others believe that "In the last days saith God, I will pour out my Spirit upon all flesh, and they shall dream dreams, see visions and prophecy," as recorded in the Second of Acts. We know when Caleb and Joshua visited the pomised land they gave a correct report and proved it by bringing some of the fruit and were permitted to dwell in it, while the rest brought an evil report and no fruit and were not permitted to visit it again, nor they that accepted their report. So it is with those who try to cry down the voice of the Spirit.

If my Holy Ghost lost his gift of speech I would send him to a mute asylum and try to get him cured. The trouble of those who cry down Spiritual gifts is, they have no Spirit to talk to them. When He comes He will bring His gifts with Him. It may be healing or exhortation prophecy, or visions, but what it is accept, and as Paul says, "Covet earnestly the best gifts." A lady told me she had a gift of visions but did not want them, as the teacher she was following did not wish her to, as she had them herself. But I think neither see them now. Another said she was afraid of being led astray by them. I heard a Free Methodist minister say the Spirit did not use dreams and visions, but if people wanted dreams let them eat a hearty supper before retiring. His member, a spiritual lady, kept a boarding house, and one of her boarders stole an overcoat. He was suspected and the house was seached in vain, when she dreamed it was hidden under the floor in the garret, and there found it. Here we have theory and experience. I attended another meeting the same day, when the minister took the same subject and said that sometimes the Lord taught us by the means of dreams and visions. Well, the tree is known by its fruit, and the fruits of the Spirit are evidence of His presence. I could relate enough such experience that has come under my notice to fill a small volume. In 1803, Joseph Hoag, a Quaker preacher, saw a vision while working in the field, in which first the division in his church, which occurred nine years later was revealed, then divisions in other churches and their worldliness, then the great Civil war and the overthrow of slavery and the setting up of antichrist's kingdom in this country. A sister-in-law was converted, after which I urged her to seek the abiding comforter. Soon she dreamed she was climbing a very steep and rickety stairway, which was covered with snow and ice, so she had to climb on her hands and knees. They were very high and difficult. She kept looking up, for it is not safe to rest our eyes on the world while we are traveling heavenward. Bunyan stopped his ears and cried: Life! Life! She reached the top and found herself in a beautiful park, more beautiful than she had ever seen and as extensive every way as the eye could reach, and she was on the very top and could see no place higher than where she stood.

After a while she began to give way to the pleasures of the world, and she had another dream. She was climbing up the same stairs again, but not looking up, but thought she could find an easier way to get up. So she went down and found another staircase of broad and beautiful marble steps, and said, "I can climb up here so much easier." So she started, but found it did not lead to the same place.

A friend who had many remarkable dreams, dreamed that none but Jacksonions would obtain the Kingdom. Jackson was a man with an iron will and would do what he thought was right if the whole world opposed him. A man that is carried away by every wind of doctrine or influence from doing what he knows to be right by others will not get there. After he has done all he must stand. Spurgeon says the man who will not in the least change the message that the Lord gave him to deliver to please the greatest man or to draw the largest congregation, will move the world, and that any man will move the world that will not let the world move him. No man can lead another into the Kingdom. Each one has got to get the Spirit for himself and follow Him. But human agencies may teach and encourage him.

Christ will never look on the church books to see who are his, for he will not take the nominal church to himself, but a people out of the churches whose name are written in heaven, and the farther any one gets from church creeds and bonds the nearer they will be to the Kingdom. First the blade, which is conversion, then the ear, which is receiving the Spirit, which, if followed, will lead to perfection.

which is the full corn in the ear. Then comes the glorious harvest of the end of the world, for the full truth is not to be preached until then. Our theological colleges are a great hindrance to the advancement of Christ's Kingdom, for men do not go to learn what the Holy Ghost teaches nor what the Bible says, but what man teaches and how to twist the Bible to fit their creed. I knew an old minister who commenced preaching when young, with but little education, and was successful in winning many souls, but after he had preached a few years he went to college, and it turned him out a very polished preacher, and he grew old in the service, but he is said to not have been instrumental in a single conversion after his education. Another took the Guide to Holiness and preached holiness when but a youth, and was soon able to baptise 250 converts. Afterward he renounced it and preached against the gifts of the Spirit to a fuller extent than I ever heard any other, and I doubt if he can find a person who has been converted by his preaching in the last 20 years. He is still preaching. The Holy Spirit honors those who honor Him. I was converted 25 years before I was taught to seek the Holy Spirit, but when I learned that there was another blessing for me I sought and found it, and with Bishop Taylor I can say since then, I have been growing, growing, growing. I visited a relative in Brooklyn who had been a professor 25 years and asked her if she had grown in grace any since her conversion. She said, not a bit. I told her to get the Spirit and let Him teach her. I called a year later and found her aglow with the Spirit, and to my question she said she was growing, and it was the happiest year of her life. If you have not the spirit of Christ you are none of his. Seek earnestly the Spirit until He reveals Himself to you.

THIRD STEP.

Holy Men of Old.

I am not an advocate of hero worship; those men whom the world has called great because of their achievement in battle are no more to be compared to that class of men whom I choose to honor than a molehill is to be compared to the mighty Alps. For they were great! Not like Caesar, stained with blood; but only great as they were good. They were the men we should delight to honor, who for the sake of God's truth were not afraid to suffer that they could have part with Him who preferred a crown of thorns to a royal diadem and a rugged cross to all of the kingdoms which the serpent had to give, and will find one who will accept. These men chose peril, nakedness, the sword, imprisonment, torture of the most excruciating kind that evil genius could devise, which was a living death; such as standing on redhot iron until their feet were burned off; their flesh raked with iron combs until their skin was nearly all off and then covered with salt and hanged by the thumbs with the truth rather than have all the honors that an empire could give with error. I refer to the fathers of the church who lived during the first three centuries, which is called the Anti-Nicene period, or the time between Christ and the Council of Nice. That was the glorious period of the church. Christ had left to the world through His disciples a perfect religion. While without was fighting, persecution and death, within was a peace that the world could neither give nor take away, and a brotherly love that knew no bounds. Well might they fall on Paul's neck and weeping cover him with kisses on taking leave of him. These men did not speak their own words, but spake and wrote as they were moved by the Holy Ghost. Think you that the inspired writings are enclosed in the lids of our Bible? I tell you, no. Our Bible was compiled after the decline of the church by uninspired men, from which James and Revelations and Hebrews were excluded for a time.

In 1851 in a Convent on Mount Sinai a manuscript bible was found, supposed to be the oldest in existence. It contained beside what is in our Bible, the Epistle of Barnabas, in 21 chapters, and the three remarkable books called the Shepherd of Hermas, which was the most popular of any books during the first four centuries, and are without question inspired and teach the deep, rich truth of the Kingdom. Hermas, the author, lived in Rome and Paul salutes him in Romans, 16:14. Why should not the Epistle of Barnabas be received as well as those of Paul? He also was numbered with the Apostles and was in the work before him, and was numbered with the seventy disciples that Christ sent out, and the Fathers quote from his as well as Hermas the same as they do from Paul's. Barnabas suffered martyrdom not long after he separated from Paul. As John Mark tells us. Clemment of Rome must not be overlooked. He was converted by the preaching of Barnabas and became Peter's companion and was noted for his earnestness and deep piety. He left four valuable epistles. The two on virginity are very important. He was Bishop of Rome.

The holy Polycarp was a disciple of the Apostle John, and is spoken of with much reverence by several of the Fathers. The account of his martyrdom is given by those who witnessed it. " As the flames blazed forth with great fury, we, who witnessed it, beheld a great miracle, for the fire shaped itself in the form of an arch and he appeared within as gold or silver in a furnace. Moreover we perceived such a sweet odor coming from the pile as if frank-incense had been smoking there. At length, when these wicked men perceived that he could not be burned, they commanded an executioner to go near and pierce him through with a dagger, when there came forth a dove and a great quantity of blood so that the fire was extinguished." The same writers called him a prophet and said all that he said had or would come to pass.

There are records of several of the Apostolic Church that, like Daniel and his three friends, neither fire nor wild beasts had the power to harm. Saint John was also cast into a caldron of boiling oil and sustained no harm. God is not a respecter of persons and would not have so miraculously preserved them without cause. That reason will be perfectly clear when we understand what the mystery of God is, as none of the thousands of just men who suffered since the mystery was lost were thus preserved. Among the former was a young heathen woman named Thakely, who was both preserved from fire and wild beasts after her conversion by the preaching of Paul. A very interesting account of her life and miraculous preservation is given in a book entitled: "Acts of Paul and Thakely;" which is spoken of and commended by the early Fathers.

Justin Martyr, as the Holy Martyr is called, gives no uncertain sound. His two pleas for the Christians, addressed to the Emperor and Roman Senate, are very important, as they show the mode of worship and practices of the Christians of his day and shows the injustice of their persecution and the falseness of the charges against them. He gives conclusive proof that the mystery that is not now publicly taught anywhere was taught and followed in the church in his day and the persecution it caused. His plea availed him nothing, as he became a victim of the martyrdom that he tried to save from others. The exact date of his writing is not known, but it must have been near the time of Paul, as he speaks of a petition being sent to Felix, the Governor, for religious liberty, and we know that he imprisoned Paul for two years and was Governor but ten years. He wrote, also, other important church papers, among which was the dialogue with Trypho, the Jew.

Ignatius was a contemporary with Polycarp, an officer in the church. He wrote a dozen or more epistles to the churches, Polycarp and others. But like Jehu, had more zeal than knowledge and desired to show his zeal for the Lord, so he desired to make a grand sacrifice to the Lord, as he said he was not perfect and thought his martyrdom would make him so, and went to the Roman tribunal and declared himself a Christian and desired to be fed to the lions, thinking by digesting him would make up that which was lacking of the sufferings of Christ. So he served them for a hearty dinner. It is clear that he was ignorant of the mystery by which he could have been perfect without sacrificing his life, as Paul did. See Colossians 1: 21-29. "While there is a great reward for those who are persecuted for righteousness sake, we have no right to seek it, for if we do we are no better than self murderers." The writers of the martyrdom of Polycarp tell of two men who voluntarily gave themselves up but when they saw the fierceness of the beasts they recanted and offered sacrifices to idols.

Origen, the son of Leonides, a Holy Christian martyr, who lived from 185 to 254, belongs to that class that Spurgeon describes as soaring up like a rocket and coming down like the stick. He received his instructions from his venerable father and accepted all of the mystery of the kingdom. His father suffered when he was a youth and he was willing to share the same fate, but his mother persuaded him not to, so he recanted the most important of all truths and so saved his miserable life at the expense of his spiritual. One step downward opened the way for more. Having lost the Spirit he was left to drift like a ship without sail or rudder. He denied the inspiration of the gospels, for which he was expelled from the church, and it is said that he finally recanted the whole Christian faith. The amusing part of the story is that all modern theologians praise him for errors and condemn him for his great virtue. They fail to see the deep truth of the mystery connected with his life. He was a man of much learning and ability, and they class him among the highest of the Fathers, while I give him the lowest place. His writings are numerous, but a small portion of them have been translated and published.

Clement of Alexandria lived over 100 years later than Clement of Rome, or from 153 to 217. His writings fill over 400 double column pages and are very interesting, although 23 pages that would to me be the most important are printed in Latin only, and I am unable to read them, but hope to soon be able to have them translated. He held some important truths not taught in the modern church, but I do not know that it was not mixed with error, or how he stood on the mystery.

Montanus appeared in the Church about 160. He left no writings, and what we know of him we learn from others. Bishop supremacy had begun to rise in the church, and the bishops ruled that they were the supreme head and must be obeyed in all things, while he taught that the Holy Spirit was the supreme power in the church and must be obeyed in preference to the bishops, and if obeyed, all of the prophetic and miraculous power of the apostolic age would return to the church. Had the church followed his teachings instead of the bishops it would not have fallen with the bishops. He claimed to be a prophet with a good reason, for he took the only way to get the spirit of prophecy.

Tertulien in his book against Praxeas, who denied the Trinity, claiming there was but one God and he only was born of the Virgin and suffered, says: "After the Bishop of Rome had acknowledged the prophetic gifts of Montanus, Presco and Maximilla, and in consequence of the acknowledgement had bestowed his peace on the churches of Asia and Phrygia. Praxeas by importunity urging false accusations against the prophets themselves and their churches and insisting on the authority of the bishop's predecessors in the see, compelling him to recall the pacific letter which he had issued, as well as to desist from his purpose of acknowledging the said gifts. By this Praxeas did a twofold service for the devil at Rome. He drove away prophecy, and he brought in heresy. He put to flight the Paraclete (Holy Spirit), and he crucified the Father." Here we have the germ that finally overthrew the spirit and essence of the Apostolic Church, and this unitarian spirit of heresy grew until Montanus and his adherents were expelled from the church, among which was Tertulian, the greatest light and glory of his century. Although this did not occur until about the end of the second century, or a century after the death of the last surviving apostle, who died at the age of 120 (if he died, as like Moses, his sepulcher was never found). In denying His gifts they virtually deny the spirit, for His only service is to give gifts unto men, and does not the spirit of Praxism rule the churches of to-day? Let a man come in claiming the spirit of prophecy and try to teach any other doctrine than that laid down in their prescribed creeds and see if he will not share the fate of Montanus and his men. Recently I heard of a minister who was forced to resign his charge for preaching that we are advancing near the time of the end. After the expulsion of these holy men (which is the first case of persecution for the sake of truth by the church recorded), they formed themselves in an independent church, which existed until the 5th or 6th century.

Tertullian! What about him? Language is inadequate; at least any that I can utter. I can say with the poet:

" Too high is the theme for my harp's lowly numbers,
Yet fain would twine me a wreath for that name,
That proudly stands forth in the tablet of glory,
Unsullied by faction, untarnished by guile,
The loftiest theme for the bard's raptured story."

He lived from 145 to 220. His writings fill about 800 large, double column pages of the Anti-Nicene Fathers, and there appears to be no point of spiritual truth untouched by him, yet a number of his works have been lost. Bishop Coxe, D. D., the American editor of the " Fathers," can not be expected to indorse his Montanus views (as he was a bishop and believed in bishop supremacy), commends him at one moment and condemns him the next. He compares him with the heretic Tatian, who is unworthy to be mentioned with him, and says, " In speaking of Tatian I laid the foundation of what I wish to speak of Tertullian. Let God only be their judge; let us gratefully recognize the debt we owe to them. Let us read them as we read the works of King Solomon." When he says something to broad and grand for Coxe's narrow mind, he adds in a note, " Montanism appears here," when he is writing on a subject that Montanus was never opposed on. It might be said of him, he told the truth, the whole truth and nothing but the truth.

If you want to know the practices of the church in his day, read Tertullian. If you want to know about the mode and confessions used in baptism, read Tertullian. If you want to know how Peter got the keys, read Tertullian. If you want to know if the sick were healed by the prayer of faith, read Tertullian. If you would know the mystery of Christ, read Tertullian. If you would learn of the second baptism, read Tertullian. And so I might go on to the end of the chapter. Yet, strange as it may appear, this old soldier of Christ was allowed to keep his liberty and die at an advanced age in his own home in those days of peril, and it can only be accounted for by his wisdom and shrewdness. When he wanted to say things that were forbidden to be published to the world, he addressed them to his wife, for a man is not supposed to be restricted in what he says to his wife, and if some one else gets hold of it that is their business, not his. Cyprian was said to be his disciple and lived and wrote his 82 epistles 40 or 50 years later, but was a different man, as he taught supremacy of the bishops, but not a universal bishop, but that each was supreme in his own district. He shows that error and superstition had crept in and that salvation was impossible outside of the pale of the church, and is the first one that mentions infant baptism. Tertullian would have said something about it in his lengthy articles on baptism if it had been practiced then, as he speaks of the baptism of children and recommends that it be deferred, and shows that sprinkling is not practiced in the church, but is practiced by stealth outside, and calls it stealing a march on God. Cyprian wrote about 250 A. D. Besides his epistles he left his treatises and other writings.

Among the last of the holy men who ruled the church was Peter, the martyr, who, like his namesake, was filled with holy zeal and endured persecution and spent years in exile and concealment. He was dearly beloved by his church, who were ready at all times to lay down their life for him. They had short periods of religious liberty when he would be restored to his charge, for he was a bishop; when it was over he would have to flee. He was also persecuted by another bishop who could not accept his holy teaching. He was finally condemned and imprisoned, when hundreds of his friends surrounded his prison and prevented his execution by watching day and night. When they decided to bring an army to overpower his friends and when he heard it he told the soldiers they might come by night and make a hole in the wall and he would come out and they could fulfill their orders, which they did, leaving his friends watching an empty prison, as they did not know of his execution until morning. He did this to save the lives of his friends, which was commendable. He was a prophet and foretold that two of his successors in office would soon share his fate, after which the church would have peace, which was fulfilled. Christ appeared to him in prison with his garments torn so as to expose his nudeness and said Arias had torn them, and that two men would come to him that day to urge him to reinstate him in the church, for he had been expelled, but not to do it, and to send word to his successor to not do it, which was fulfilled. He was beheaded A. D. 312.

Arius was the man that up to his time created the greatest tumult in the church, and on his account the Council of Nice was called. He was a Unitarian, denying that Christ was equal to or the same in substance as the Father, and had by his eloquence and learning drawn many to his opinion, but was expelled at a council at Alexandria and afterwards reinstated at a council at Bethynia, and Constantine called another to Nice, over which he presided. There were 318 bishops present, and all but two decided against him. The Emperor passed an edict banishing him and commanding all of his writings to be burned under pain of death. Three years later the Emperor was persuaded by Arius' friends to recall him, and in 330 the Emperor ordered that he be reinstated, but the bishops refused, and the tumult continued until 336, when he got the Emperor to pass an edict that he should be received in the church and receive the communion from the hand of the bishop, and his friends made a triumphal march towards the church, but Arius was taken with a violent hemorrhage and died before he reached it.

I have expanded this article beyond the limit I alloted to myself, but time is too short to speak of all of these holy men and it seems as I have but just begun, as their writings fill 24 volumes in the Edinburgh edition, or eight large volumes of 600 to 800 double column pages in the American edition, and were not published in this country until about ten years ago, by A. Cleveland Coxe, D. D., Bishop of Buffalo, who died last July. He has rendered a great service to his country, but I fear that his greatest inducement was the profit, as they are only sold in complete sets, and the first price was $3 per volume and $2.50 for an index volume that was added; then he raised the price to $3.50, then to $4. Chas. Scribner's Sons, New York, now publish them in 10 volumes for $20. I count them the most important of all of the books published to-day, as they give the teachings of the united church founded by Christ and the Apostles, and no modern work on church theology is to be compared with it, as much is written by inspiration.

The death of Arius did not put an end to Arianism, for he had made many converts. Constantine, the first Christian emperor so called, had become one and denied the divinity of Christ, so they had a Christianity at Rome without a Christ. His son and successor also embraced it. After him idolatry filled the throne. When the devil used Praxeas to wrest the spirit and His gifts from the church, he sapped its foundation and the rest was easy.

While Cyprian taught important truths he also taught errors, claiming there was no salvation outside of the regular church; while he admitted for baptism, immersion, pouring and sprinkling, as well as being the first to endorse infant baptism, he declared it invalid if administered outside of the regular church, and such must be rebaptised before they could be admitted. While the Nicene council decided the Arean heresy correctly, they locked the door against the entrance of the church into the kingdom of Christ and opened it to creed-making, and made the first of which there is any record, as the so called Apostles' creed cannot be traced back farther than the fourth century, and the earliest copies make no mention of the descent into hell. When men make a rule to govern the faith of mankind they relieve the great teacher, the spirit, of any further service. Creed-making was easier begun than ended, and all were not willing to accept the Nicene creed, so they made another, and that was not better accepted, and so creeds were multiplied until there were soon not less than eleven, and that number has been multiplied many times since.

When the spirit's gift and the mystery of the inner Christ life was wrested from the church, its fall was rapid. When the external persecution ended, the internal war increased, and peace was for all time past taken from the church. The Arian dispute lasted through several centuries. Maritins, the Emperor, A. D. 590, commanded Gregory, the Great, bishop of Rome, to obey John, bishop of Constantinople, but he would not abide that any bishop should be universal above all the rest. It is said of Gregory that he was the basest of all his predecessors and the best of all his successors, which shows its rapid decline. History says, in the year 1000 religion was wholly decayed to what it was in former times; and from the year 300 to that time, many dark institutions were set up in the church of the pretended Christians, insomuch that it became midnight for darkness and the Popes began to draw the sword in defence of Peter's keys after every trace of them had been wrested from the church and lost. The Pope claims to have them, and I demand of him, or his representatives or followers, what they are and what Peter did to earn so great a reward, and if he is doing the same

Many of the Anti-Nicene Fathers wrote from inspiration, and if we are filled with the spirit He will enable us to discern between the spiritual and natural man.

FOURTH STEP.

Imputed Righteousness Answered.

I recently listened to a sermon from "No man that wareth entangleth himself with the affairs of this life that he may please him who hath called him to be a soldier." 2 Tim. 2: 4. From this text the speaker preached imputed righteousness and told the oft repeated story of the man that was drafted in the late civil war and hired a substitute to take his place, who fell in battle, after which he was again drafted, but claimed that he was dead to the government as his substitute had died for him, and by this illustrates Christ's death for us. We will illustrate this substitute business a little, as I fail to see any of it in the text, for those who become soldiers do not furnish substitutes to do their fighting for them. God forbid that I should make this a personal attack upon the preacher in person, for the doctrine of imputed righteousness is one of the most unscriptural and dangerous doctrines taught, yet it is held by all christian and catholic denominations (so called), yet it has no Bible foundation. The preacher quoted was more excusable than most preachers, for she was a woman, and her sex are excused from engaging in warfare by both civilized and heathen nations, and are expected to do all of their fighting through substitutes.

If this man had died in his substitute why did not his widow apply and get the pension due a soldier's widow, as no law can compel a woman to live with a dead man. If a man went to court the widow, I think he would run against a very lively corpse. No brave soldier filled with love of country would, when his country was in peril, sit in his home and send a foreigner to fight in his room for fear that he would not be as valiant as himself, as the government would not accept citizens as substitutes as they were liable to be drafted themselves, and the only inducement of the hireling would be the price of his hire, and his greatest ambition would be to save his life and flee when he saw the wolf coming, like the hireling in the parable, for he would not be fighting for his country, his altar, or his home. In the Revolution the English hired the Hessian soldiers to whip us into subjection. Did they do it? He had given the life of an alien for his country and had no more to give, while he spent his time with his wife and orphan (?) children. What a brave soldier! He surely deserves a crown. Would we ever have saved our country's flag with such patriotism? When Patrick Henry said in his ever living speech, "Give me liberty or give me death," did he mean the death of an alien, unknown to him? Some foreigners like La Fayette, De Kalb and Steuben, have, by their self-denial and courage, proved valiant soldiers and were raised to the head of armies. Suppose that had been the fortune of the substitute, could the principal then say: You have earned all of these honors in my name for me while I have been living at my ease in safety, but now I will take the place at the head of the army and you can retire; you have shed some of your blood for my country and I will wear the scars; you have lost an arm but I will wear the empty sleeve; you have earned a pension, I will receive it; you won a crown of glory, I will wear it. Would there be any justice or equity or reason in it? Certainly not. Let him who earned the crown wear it.

It is even so with those who presume to attain to Christ's righteousness and kingdom by imputing to themselves Christ's righteousness that he earned by his suffering. Does a brave soldier remain behind and let his general brave the dangers alone? Neither will a general give to a deserting soldier the honor he earns. Did Christ teach imputed righteousness when He said, " Let him who will come after me take up his cross and follow me." Or Paul, when he said, " So fight I to keep my body under, lest while I am preaching to others I myself become a castaway." Or the text or Peter, when he said: " Since Christ suffered in the flesh for us, arm yourselves with the same mind, for he who has suffered in the flesh has ceased from sin." Or James, who said, " Be afflicted." Christ suffered to show us how he opened the doors, and there is no other way for us to the Kingdom but by suffering. Ye have not yet resisted unto blood striving against sin, and if you do not " ye are bastards and not sons," says Paul, and will not be admitted into Christ's presence, or the Kingdom, for no bastard ever inherited a crown. Tertulien who is the grandest of the early fathers, said, " He who is afraid to suffer will have no part with him who suffers, but he who is not afraid to suffer will be made perfect in suffering, for he who has suffered in the flesh has ceased from sin," says Peter. " And if ye suffer ye shall reign with him," says Paul to Timothy. Generals take to themselves the glory of their victory, or share it with their valiant soldiers, but not with deserters. And it is promised reward that urges them to risk their lives. Christ endured the cross, despising the shame, and is now set down at the right hand of the throne of God, and done it for the glory that was set before Him. As in Rom. 1: 4, " Christ declared to be the Son of God, with power according to the spirit of holiness." How did he get this power? By the resurrection from the dead, or in other words, by his victory over sin and death that gave Him all power on earth and in heaven, as He tells us. Is there any righteousness for us in this? Does not He tread the winepress alone? And does not the victory and reward belong to Him alone? Who would, if they could, rob Him of any of it? Yet He has vouchsafed for us the same victory, the same honors, the same crown and power if we fight the same battle and prove ourselves to be as valiant soldiers. Did Paul presume on Christ's righteousness when he said, " I have fought the good fight, I have kept the faith, therefore, there is laid up for me a crown of righteousness which the Lord, the righteous Judge, shall give me at that day." Before he wrote, " So fight I not as one that breath the air, but to keep my body under lest while I am preaching to others I myself become a castaway." So we see Paul was looking for a reward for service rendered, the same as a servant is looking for the wages of his hire, only the reward is so great as not to be compared with the service required, for Paul says, " The sufferings of this present time is not to be compared with the glory that shall be revealed in us." If we get the Holy Spirit and follow Him instead of the teachings of men. He will tell us what service and sufferings will be acceptable to God.

To illustrate, suppose A has some labor that he wants performed, on which there was a large profit. B and C takes it. B performed his part and receives his part of the price. C goes to the Judge to have him compel A to pay him the other half, and states his grievance.

J. Have you performed your part of the service?

C. Me! Service! Why, Judge, what do you take me for? I am no servant, but a gentleman; beside the labor is degrading.

J. Are you more of a gentleman than B was, who performed his part?

C. I do not know as I am.

J. Was not the reward so much greater than the amount of service as not to be compared with it?

C. Certainly it was.

J. If you was not willing to do even a small service to earn a great reward, on what do you base your claim?

C. Why, on B's generosity. I thought he might do the work for me and give me the reward.

J. Did he agree to?

C. No, he said he would show me how, but I did not give him a chance.

You have not a shadow of a case says the righteous Judge. I will throw it out of court. Go perform your service then you can claim your reward.

Put Christ in B's case and those who depend on Christ's righteousness for their reward in C's case, who go through the world singing, Jesus bore it all. All to him I owe. Instead of

> Shall Jesus bear the cross alone
>   And all the world go free?
> No, there's a cross for every one,
>   And there's a cross for me.
>
> The consecrated cross I'll bear,
>   Till Christ shall set me free,
> And then go home, a crown to wear;
>   For there's a crown for me.

Is not our God, the God of nature, of equity, justice and common sense, and does not imputed righteousness oppose all? Would there be any sense in punishing the good boy to make the bad boy good? Who would care to live in a country where the life of a substitute was taken and the murderer allowed to go free? If God is the author of imputed righteousness, His kingdom is divided against itself and cannot stand.

O, for the wing of the morning that I might fly to the utermost parts of the earth, and the voice of the seven thunders, that I might tell the theologians that we have a God who has common sense, and when Paul said, "We have the mind of Christ," he did not mean we were a set of idiots. Also Young in his "Teachings of the Bible" says, "How we are accountable for Adam's sin is a mystery that I never heard explained." I honor his honesty, but pity his ignorance. If he knew what his sin was he would know how it affected him and how it could be atoned for, which, if done, would place him where Adam was before the fall.

I saw a catechism used in a German Sunday School. All I could read of it was the illustrations. The first was a huge snake coiled up in an appletree picking the apples and giving them to naked Eve, who handed them to nude Adam. If Esop could not have manufactured a better fable than the snake story he would never have got a record. But Eve ate the apples just the same, but I have not room to enlarge on it here. Tens of thousands have grown old trying to write and tell the story and have not told it, and do you expect me to tell it in one brief sermon? "He bore our sins in his own body on the tree," and like passages seems to teach imputed righteousness at first thought. and the lines

"Was it for sins that I had done,
He groaned upon the tree."

are misleading as though my own sins committed more than one thousand years after He suffered would add a bit to his sufferings. or that the sins of the bloody Nero, who painted the streets of Rome red with the blood of the martyred christians and lighted it with his human torches. would have caused Christ to suffer any more than the sins of that good boy who "could not tell a lie." Sinful acts are caused by sinful thoughts. An idiot, or infant, who is incapable of thinking cannot sin, and sinful thoughts arise from a sinful nature. If we crucify or destroy our sinful nature we will have no more sinful thoughts and will become children of God, for God says, "He who is born of God cannot commit sin." Can God sin? Certainly not. And when we have the mind of Christ we cannot. That is just what Christ came to teach us. He took our nature that he received from fallen Adam, kept it under subjection, and finally crucified it, which again made Him one with God, and told us to do the same. All kinds of anathemas have been hurled at Paul because the Holy Spirit said by his mouth, "I will not allow a woman to teach." While I do not deny that women who do their duty will have the first places in the Kingdom, but there are certain services from which women are excused, for when He said, "Whom the Lord loveth he chasteneth, and scourgeth every son whom he receiveth." He did not mean daughter. So, as they were excused from receiving the severe penalty of the law, they were unqualified to teach it, for a general must lead his army. But when the Council of Nicae, 325 after Christ, wrested the most vital part or substance of the Gospel from the Church and left only the shadow by the decree of that council, the men became as effeminate as the women, and the latter as capable of teaching the shadow as the men, and their assistance to God's teachers and prophets will be accepted of God.

To the intelligent mind it is more amusing than edifying to hear one attempt to explain what he does not understand, and especially when he tries to explain the existence of a theory that cannot exist; for imputed righteousness is in violation of God's laws and consequently cannot exist. It reminds me of the colored gentleman's effort to explain the working of the telegraph.

Jack—Can you 'splain how they send letters on the telegraph?

Sam—Sartin, sure. 'Spose I could work on it if I didn't know all 'bout it.

Jack—'Splain it then, for I want to know very much.

Sam—'Spose there was a long dog that reached from here to New York—

Jack—But there ain't no such long dog.

Sam—If you don't 'spose there is such a long dog I can't 'splain.

Jack—Well, 'spose then, but I never seed such a long dog.

Sam—Well, 'spose his tail is here and his nose in New York. I steps on his tail here and he barks in New York. See!

Jack—O, yes; but how do you work the telegraph?

Sam—I digs the holes to set the poles in.

Of all the theologians who have lived since the Apostolic age, I place John Bunyan in the first rank, for he waded deeper in the mysteries of God than any other, but when he attempted to ford the slough of imputed righteousness he got far beyond his depth, as he was honest enough to admit, for he says in the commencement of his article on the subject, "This is one of the greatest mysteries in the world, namely, that a righteousness that resides with a person in heaven should justify me on earth." That is what I call, and that rightly, the mysterious act of our redemption in Christ's sufferings as a common though, a particular person, and as a sinner, though always completely righteous. This is also so mysterious that it goes beyond the reach of all men to comprehend it, that one particular man should represent all the elect in himself and that the most righteous should die by the hands of a just and holy God is a mystery of the greatest depth.

And now I come to show you how the elect are

concerned therein—that is, in the mysterious act of this most blessed one, and this will make this act yet more mysterious to you. We will not attempt to follow Bunyan farther, or at present help him out of his maise, for his attempt to solve what he either admits or acknowledges is so deep a mystery to him will not be to our edification. Paul says, "We have the mind of Christ." John says, "Ye need not that any man teach you, for ye have the anointing and ye know all things." The early fathers did not have this error to contend with, for it was not taught in the Apostolic Church, but I will give a single extract from Tertullian, the Solomon of the fathers who wrote 200 A. D. Speaking of the resurrection, he says, "How absurd, and in truth, how unjust, and in both respects, how unworthy of God for one substance to do the work and another to reap the reward; that this flesh of ours should be torn by martyrdom and another wear the crown; or, on the other hand, that this flesh of our should wallow in uncleanness and another receive the condemnation! Is it not better to renounce all faith at once, in the hope of the resurrection, than to trifle with the wisdom and justice of God." This was not written against any Christians, as none at that date accepted the doctrine, but a semi-heathen sect called Valentimans, after their founder, Valentine, who created thirty gods.

If you will bear with me a little I will make these mysteries so plain that the blind can see if they will, but do not expect it all in a single sermon, for to bring one from a dungeon to the glare of the noonday sun, the light would blind. So with spiritual truth. I know I am saping the foundation of the modern church, but the quicker the sandy foundation is removed the better, so we can plant it on the rock. So let us first remove the rubbish that modern theologians have built on so we can get down to the corner stone. The Nicaen Council, held 325 A. D., made two mistakes. First, by their creed that told what part of Christ's teachings they should accept instead of all. Second, the greater one, by teaching the part they must reject, which was the most vital, and removed it from the rock to imputed righteousness.

I will now close with Peter's benediction: "The God of all grace, who has called us unto his eternal glory by Jesus Christ, after that ye have suffered a while, make you perfect, establish, strengthen and settle you." Amen.

FIFTH STEP.

THINK.—Think On These Things—Phil. 4: 8.

In dividing the text we will first consider the first word. Have you ever thought that if people would only stop and consider we would have a very much better world. The sinner would withhold his hand if he would think that his acts were seen by a terrible and revengeful God, who said to Ephraim, "They consider not in their hearts that I remember all their wickedness. They are all before my face." The Psalmist says, "Now consider this thou that forget God, lest I tare you in pieces and there be none to deliver. Compare the few days of this miserable life with the never ending eternity. Will the deceitful promises of sinful pleasure compensate for an eternity doomed to never-ending anguish and despair? Before it is too late think on these things." They are not the only class that needs to think, but the religious professors as well, from the lowest subject to the highest, Protestant officials as well as he that graces the Papel chair.

Was it not the want of thought that has divided the holy church planted by Christ and the Apostles into a thousand shreds? Are we not more ready to imbibe the thoughts of others than to think for ourselves? The convert makes no pretentions to know what he believes until he decides which church he will unite with, and then he will go to the minister to ascertain what he believes, and what he tells him swallows like the swine does his food and then goes to sleep until the time for the next rations. The

Apostle Barnabus says in his epistle that those who meditated were typified in the clean beasts that raised and ruminated the cud after they had eaten, while those that did not, like the unclean. Has not the creed, the cathecism, the class-book and the prayer-book more influence on the minds of the religious world to-day than the Bible? I met a christian worker who held the unscriptural belief that the Holy Spirit was a woman. I tried to convince her of her error. She said she would believe it if a thousand persons said it was not so. I asked her if the spirit revealed it to her. She said, no, but her minister did, and what he said she would believe if a thousand denied it. You may think her case peculiar, but it is not, for I know of errors just as unscriptural held by large denominations, and no amount of reasoning will convince them of their error.

I will mention one which is held by half of the Christian world and is found in the so called Apostle's Creed, which says Christ suffered under Pontius Pilate, was buried, descended into hell. Of course there is much of the creed that all Christians can accept, but we have no right to call it the Apostles' unless we have proof that they wrote it. There is no mention of it in the Bible. I have carefully gone over the over 5,000 pages of the fathers of the church of the first three centuries, and find they quote from every chapter and nearly every verse of the new testament, besides from four other books that were then in the new testament, but has been thrown out, and find in them no mention of such creed, nor any mention of Christ's descent into hell, which part of the creed I wish to consider, unless I consider an aprocryphal book called the descent into hell, by Nicodemus, of which there is three versions, of which no two agree, and no mention is made of it until the 13th century. The story is as wild and as unscriptural as Jules Verne's journey to the moon. Chambers' Encyclopedia says the earliest account we have of its origin is from Rufinus, a historian compiler of the fourth century. No great weight belongs to his testimony, for he is no historical authority. There were in the early church different forms of the creed. "He descended into hell, and communion of saints," is supposed to have been interpolated according to later notions.

The earliest creed of which there is positive proof is the Nicene creed, which was made at that council 325 A. D. This Gibbon tells us was the beginning of creed making, but not the beginning of the end, for all would not accept it, and so other councils met and made others, so in a short time there was not less than eleven different creeds, and since then that number has been multiplied many times.

While the creed has been repeated in thousands of churches every Sunday for nearly a thousand years, I never heard a minister make any remarks about the descent into hell, nor read anything from theologians on the subject, but Martin Luther, and he said he could not understand what Christ went to hell for unless it was to commence to chain the devil, as if it would take two thousand years to accomplish the job and the angel was not able to do it alone. We read in Rev. 12: 10, that the devil is before the throne of God accusing the saints day and night, but immediately after the first resurrection, which is still future, he and his angels will be cast down to the earth, which is not hell (though many have tried to turn it into one), where he will remain three years and a half, after which he will be chained and cast into the abyss, where he will remain a thousand years, and that is not hell. So if Christ went to hell to chain him He did not find him there. Did He go to preach to the angels that sinned? Judge says, "And the angels that kept not their first estate but left their own habitation, he hath left in everlasting chains under darkness unto the judgment of the great day." So they are not in hell, neither are the wicked dead, for they are in their graves and will not be raised until the end of the thousand years, as we read in Rev. 20:5. If neither the devil nor his angels nor the wicked dead are in hell, who did Christ go down to bind or preach to? Again, all will agree that hell will be a place of punishment for condemned sinners, and they will not be tried and judged until the day of judgment, which is still future. What would you think of a court that would hang a man accused of murder and have his trial after, to see if he is guilty, or even send him to State prison? Would you not call such a judge unjust and unworthy to hold his office? Is God more unjust than man? I ask the Christian world what Christ went to hell for?

Once more. If I should say there is no hell I would have all the theologians upon me. I believe that the wicked shall be cast into hell with all the nations that forget God, but they will not be until they are judged, and then there will be time enough to prepare a place for them. What a fearful waste of brimstone it would be to keep hellfire going for 7,000 years when there was no one to be benefited by it. Would He, who would gather up the fragments that nothing be lost, be responsible for such a loss. We have a record of what was created each day of creation, but no mention of such a place. Christ said to his disciples. "I go to prepare a place for you," which place will be needed 1,000 years before the former. God said, "Behold, I make all things new." So according to his word he will have to make hell over again before he has use for it, if he made it before. Finally, Rev. 14, in speaking of them that have part in the first resurrection says they are they that follow the lamb wheresoever he goeth. If they send Christ to hell every week I do not see how they can follow Him everywhere, unless they go there themselves, and it is plain that there is no escape for them that once get to hell, for Jacob's ladder went from earth to heaven, but did not descend to hell, so they cannot escape on that. I have known some hardened sinners profane enough to send their horses and cattle to hell, but I never knew one so irreligious as to send the Saviour of the world to hell.

The descent into hell is a popeish dogma that cannot be traced beyond the darkness of the medieval ages, and those Protestant churches that broke the Papal yoke brought this relic of the abyss with its fumes of purgatory with them, and have clung to it without stopping to think of its inconsistency. Is it not strange that there has not been a thinking man in the church for a thousand years? Think on these things. But, say you, we live in a thinking age, the world has made more advancement in enlightenment, civilization and useful discoveries during the present century than it has for fives or tens of centuries previous. Certainly. The time had come to fulfill Daniel's prophecy of the closing events of the age, that knowledge should be increased, and God raised up the men and endowed them with the ability to accomplish it. Four words from one who had made the greatest achievement tells the story of the century. They were: "What hath God wrought?"

I have no confidence in man's ability if left to himself. He would soon work his ruin and become a vagabond and a fugitive on the earth. Measure to me the religious pulse of a nation and I will give the extent of its inventive ability. Without the inspiration of the Holy Spirit our thoughts are vain; but through Him we can do all things. So we should ever seek the spirit to direct our thoughts. If we do not the devil, who is an imitator of God in all things, will direct our thoughts to his advantage.

There is no doubt in my mind but what the Coren, Book of Mormon, Age of Reason, and Christian Science, falsely so called, and many others I might name, are inspired from Satan.

We will now consider God's purpose in creating man. Was it to have him for a servant? No. For Christ said, I call you not servants but friends. Again I will compel you to sit down and will gird myself and serve you. We will next consider what kind of a friend and companion God made. The Word says, "The heart is deceitful above all things and despairably wicked, who can know it!" Paul says, "The carnal mind is not subject to the law of God, neither, indeed, can be so, then they that are in the flesh cannot please God." After his wonderful conversion and receiving the Holy Spirit and preaching the Kingdom over 20 years, we find him saying, 'What I would, do I not; but what I hate, that do I. I find then a law that when I would do good evil is present with me." Did God make such a blunder in creating man to be his friend that he turned out an enemy that could not do his pleasure nor keep his law even if he wanted to? So he exclaims, "O, wretched man that I am!" After the human family had multiplied the earth was filled with violence, so it was necessary to select the best family and destroy the rest, but Noah went on a spree about as soon as he landed. Then God tried Abraham, but did not succeed much better. Then he sent his only son to teach men how to live, but they reversed the order and showed Him how to die and laid him in a grave, but not content with that, even to this present moment, send him to the lowest hell with a voice as free as they repeat the Lord's prayer.

The question for us to consider is, did God create man with such a rebellious nature and evil heart, or was it the result of the fall? All will agree it was the latter. Very well, then the effect of Adam's sin must have been such as to entirely reverse his nature and that of his descendants, for which God hid his face from the whole human race, and if God changes not, as he says, man's nature has got to be changed back before he can behold the face of his Maker. Luther says that God has been reconciled to look upon Adam's sin with impunity, and men guilty of it can return to paradise with the crime for which Adam was expelled. Make God's word true if every man is a liar. When our nature is changed back we will become children of the most High, and it will be as impossible for us to sin as it is now to refrain from sin, for John says, "Whatsoever is born of God cannot commit sin; for his seed remaineth in him and he cannot sin because he is born of God." Why? Because if we have God's nature we cannot sin more than He can. Then there is but two things for us to think out. First, what was Adam's sin that so entirely changed our nature? Second, what can we do or has been done to change our nature back? I will leave you for the present to solve these two great problems. I will make some suggestions. Will water baptism and the Lord's supper do it? No. It did not so effect Paul; and some of the worst men that I have known have received both, and some of the best neither. So it seems if we receive them we are not the better, or reject them are we the worse. I am not opposed to them, but cannot explain all in one brief sermon. If we receive no benefit they must have been given for a sign, and we ought to know what they typify. Did Christ's hanging on the cross change our nature? No. We are tempted as much as men were before. The cross is full of meaning but the present church gets no benefit because they do not understand it. Dr. Paine, of Bethel, said Christ's life was a perfect model and if we followed it we would be saved. I told him he was right. He said we gained nothing by his death. I told him we were saved by His life but became kings by the cross if we took it up, yet we gain nothing by Christ's suffering, for it is contrary to all law, both moral and physical, for one person to be benefited by the sufferings of another. Tertulien, the Solomon of the early fathers, says, "How absurd, and in truth, how unjust, and in both respects, how unworthy of God, for one substance to do the work and another reap the reward, that this flesh of ours should suffer by martyrdom and another wear the crown; or, on the other hand, that this flesh of ours should wallow in uncleanness and another receive the condemnation. Is it not better to renounce all faith in the resurrection than to trifle with the wisdom and justice of God."

When I was a student, part of my work was to solve arithmetical problems. After working one that filled the slate, I found I did not get the answer given in the book, and after going over it again failed to find any error, and concluded the answer in the book was wrong. Many theologians work the problem of salvation in the same way, and instead of conforming their faith to the simple word, they try to twist the text to conform to their views. Among this innumerable host is Alvah Hovey, D. D., L. L. D., the great Baptist commentator, who refuses to accept these plain and simple words of Christ literally, "When the gospel of the kingdom has been preached to all nations, then will the end come," because it upsets his postmillenium theory that had not a word of scripture to back it. He may be excusable for he does not know what the gospel of the Kingdom is, as he never hinted at it, and does not know the difference between being saved under the law, which is as far as the modern churches get, which means to be a subject under Christ and his brethren and dwell on the earth separated from Christ during the millenium, and exposed to another temptation when

Satan will be loosened at the end of the millenium; while to inherit the kingdom means to reign with Christ in the heavenly Jerusalem for ever, as was taught during the first three centuries of the Christian era.

When I went back to my arithmetic I found I had made a mistake in copying the example, and there was no other way than to rub my work all out and begin again; and the churches will never find the kingdom until they rub out and begin again, as they begun wrong, and produce subjects instead of kings, or bastards instead of sons. See Hebrews, 12: 8.

Many have tried to reconcile science with religion, but they have utterly failed to show how we are punishable for Adam's sin, committed 6,000 years ago, when we read that the son shall not suffer for the sin of the parent; nor show how by the death of one all died, nor how by the death of another all could be made alive; nor how by punishing the good boy (Christ), we, the bad boy, could be made good. We have an illustration in history. By the death of his great-grandfather, Louis 15th became king of France at the age of 5 years, and how to educate the young king was a very serious question, as he refused to obey his governess, as he thought kings were born to govern and not to be governed, and he did not take kindly to books, and to lay violent hands on the person of the king was an act of high treason, punishable with death, so she tried to punish him by proxy. So she called in John, a poor boy, to be his companion and schoolmate, and when the king refused to study or broke the rules, she punished John, but it does not seem to have had any better effect than Christ's sufferings has on us, for Louis 15th was one of the most immoral and worst rulers that ever disgraced the French throne. The pulpits of to-day, I see, while they pretend to herald the prince of peace, are clamoring for the blood of the poor benighted Filipinos. Write this down in your table of laws: " No true follower of the Prince of Peace can on any pretex imbue his hand in the blood of his fellow man."

The author of the laws of science, justice and equity is also the author of the laws of religion, and they will harmonize if we rightly interpret them, and if you follow me in a few sermons I will prove how it can be done without deviating from the plain literal teachings of the Bible. Finally brethren, whatsoever things are true, whatsoever things are honest, whatsoever things are just, whatsoever things are pure, whatsoever things are lovely, whatsoever things are of good report; if there be any virtue and if there be any praise.

Think on these things.

SIXTH STEP.

Final Perseverance of the Saints and Bible Twisting.

"Whosoever is born of God doth not commit sin, for his seed remaineth in him, and he cannot sin because he is born of God;" I John, 3: 9.

Methodist Lesson papers were used in a Baptist Sunday School, and the minister got hold of one on which there was the following: Q. Can a fully justified and sanctified believer be lost? A. Yes; for Paul said: "So fight I to keep my body under, lest while I am preaching to others I myself become a castaway." The minister made this the subject of a sermon, as the Baptist as well as the Presbyterians hold the doctrine of "final perseverence," or that a person once converted cannot be lost; while the Methodists hold the opposite.

He said, after repeating the question and answer, that it was a very dangerous error; but failed to state wherein the danger lay. For if I am converted and cannot be lost I fail to see how I can be lost if I wrongly think I can, and that thought would stimulate to watchfulness and service, for there must be some little reward for that. I heard another Baptist minister say in a sermon that "some held the doctrine of final perseverance and they persevered in their laziness." I know of no doctrine so promotive of laziness, and if I knew the doctrine to be true I would spend no time or money on a person that was converted; for when I go fishing I never spend any time to catch them that are in the basket, neither would I spend any time to earn the money that I had earned and put in the bank, if I had any there. But if the doctrine is wrong then they do a person a great wrong by making them believe they cannot be lost when they can, for it makes them rely on an old experience, instead of the daily witness of the spirit that they are the children of God, and makes them careless and opens the door to let the adversary in; and I fail to find a single text of scripture to support the doctrine, while those that teach the opposite are too numerous to quote. I will give one, Ezekiel 18; 20, "The soul that sinneth it shall die," and applies equally to the most hardened wretch that ever trod God's footstool as it does to Michael the Archangel or to the Son of God himself. The least sin unrepented of will bar us from Christ's presence forever. Again, in the 26th verse, "When a righteous man turneth away from his righteousness and committeth iniquity and dieth in them; for his iniquity that he hath done shall he die." Yet ye say the way of the Lord is not equal. They say this applies to them who were under the law and not to us. If it does not apply to us then the ways of God would not be equal, for if a man who has the gift of the Holy Ghost to teach him and keep him from sinning and turn his back on his former righteousness, why should he have any advantage over them who fell from less light and privileges. The doctrine is not only not taught in the Bible, but I have examined the christian literature of the first three centuries and failed to find it hinted at by any christian writer previous to John Calvin, who appears to be its discoverer and promoter, and strange to say nearly half of christendom is following his unscriptural views. The trouble is people do not think for themselves, but adopt the thoughts of others. Our preachers have got their theology from their peculiar religious schools, where they did not go to learn what the Bible says, but to twist it to fit the faith or want of faith of their church, which was founded on the opinion of some man who lived and died generations ago; and without giving the Holy Spirit a ghost of a chance to take any part in the teaching. If some preachers would cut from their Bible all that they are not willing to accept and teach literally, they would hardly have enough left to make a respectable pamphlet. I will now show you how that minister twisted himself around that text, or rather the text to fit his sectarian views. He said Paul was not afraid of being lost as he knew he could not be, for castaway did not mean lost, but only that God would remove him from the work and translate him to glory; and illustrated it with an old Roman gold coin, which when worn so it became light weight it was withdrawn from circulation and returned to the mint to be melted and made into a bright new coin; and that was what Paul was afraid would happen to him if he did not fight against the evil nature of his body. Does he pretend to say that any one can give way to the natural desire of the flesh without running any risk? If so let us eat and drink and be merry, for to-morrow we die. I fail to understand why Paul fought to prevent that which he so much desired; for he said, "To die is gain;" and again, "I desire to depart and be with Christ, which is far better." But a strange part of it is that castaway means saved, or translated into glory. O, Webster, how could you have made such a mistake, for if it does, then saved means lost, and the kings English is out of joint. If castaway means saved, then poor Paul was surely lost, for he says in 1 Cor., I1: 1: He did not cast him away.

A strange part of this sermon was that there were three Baptist preachers to hear it, all of which were loud in their praise of it and could hardly keep their seats until he was through. Which proves that the more a man twists the Bible to fit the views of his church the more he will be honored. I do not give the minister the honor of being original in so wresting God's Word, for I had heard the same arguments before. Neither do I think that he believed that he gave the true meaning, but it was Baptist theology and he must preach it to please his people. He told me that there was a place high up the spiritual ladder from which it was impossible to fall, but he made no mention of it in his sermon. We will see if we can find it.

FINAL PERSEVERENCE PROVED.

I have shown that the Calvinists are wrong in their theory of perseverence. I will also prove that the Wesleyans are more so. A shoemaker is one who makes shoes, and he is a shoemaker as long as he makes shoes, but when he ceases to make shoes he is no longer a shoemaker in fact, but he may be so by trade, for to know how to do a thing does not make one a doer of it.

We will apply this to the sinner, for as long as he sins he is a sinner, and I do not care if he belongs to a dozen churches and spends half of his time in prayer, and repents every time he sins, as long as he sins he is a sinner. But when he ceases from sinning he ceases to be a sinner and becomes a saint. I find that people who profess to be christians do not like to be called sinners, but I have to call things by their right names, and Webster will bare me out in it; and I then put sinners in two classes, the unrepentent who delights to do evil and do it with both hands and make it their boast; and the penitent who do it under uncontrollable temptation and afterwards are sorry for it and ashamed of it.

I will now go back to my text, "He who is born of God cannot commit sin." It is clear that if a saved man gets where he cannot sin he gets where he cannot be lost. So I have proved the Wesleyans wrong in saying that he can. Hark! I hear you all say, "I do not believe that, for I know that I can sin, and like Paul have to fight to keep my body under. Do you think we can get ahead of the Apostle Paul! I would like to see a man that could not sin; he must be an idiot." Not quite so fast; if your experience differs from the Bible, which is true? Let God be true though every man is a liar. I do not doubt that you can sin, and if you can you do and you are a sinner and not a saint; and I think it would trouble me now to find a saint, because all are teaching for doctrines the commandments of men, and the Holy Spirit the sanctifier has been lost sight of. Can God sin or Christ? Certainly not. When we get his nature and become one with Him and have His mind, how can we more than He? Sin is the fruits of temptation which we received from the evil one, and when we get where we cannot be tempted we will be free from sin. A parallel passage with the text is found in I John, 5, 18: "Whosoever is born of God sinneth not; but he that is begotten of God keepeth himself and the wicked one touches him not." This is the new birth of which Christ talked to Nicodemus, and over which the church stumbles by saying that it means conversion, when it means full sanctification, of which the nature of the receiver is entirely changed.

When Paul wrote Romans, 1 Corinthians and Phillippians, he had not yet obtained this experience, as he plainly tells us in Rom. 7 and 8 that he is sinning and doing the things that he hates; and in Phillippians 3, 10 to 13, he tells us that he has not suffered, by which he expects perfection. So you see the Calvanists error by trying to make apply the experience of a saint, for while Paul sinned he was a sinner and the Wesleyans try to prove by the experience of a sinner that a saint could be lost. But in Col. 1: 24, he has come to another experience:. He says: "Who now rejoice in my sufferings for you and fill up that which is behind, of the afflictions of Christ in my flesh for his body sake." That suffering, he says, was the mystery that had been hid with God from all generations; but this will be more fully explained in another sermon.

A CHALLENGE TO THE CHRISTIAN WORLD.

I am prepared to prove: 1st. That Christ came to teach men by what service they could obtain His kingdom and become joint heirs with Him in ruling it, or copartners in its government.

2d. That this mystery of Christ's kingdom was taught in the church from the apostolic age until the opening of the third century.

3d. That by the decree of the Cannal of Nicae, 325 years after Christ, all ministers holding the mystery of the kingdom were refused ordination in the church and churches of all sects; both Protestant and Catholic have adhered to it since, and the teachings of the churches have failed to bring a single man into the Kingdom or Sonship of God since, except only John Bunyan in his " Holy War," and a secret christian organization that I know but a litle about in Russia, but have been banished.

CONDITIONS.

I will prove it in public debate, with some limitation, with any number of men, not exceeding ten, of any one or different churches, either Protestant or Catholic, who will answer any question that I ask to the best of their ability, and allow me one-half of the time, and no speaker is to occupy more than 25 minutes at a time. To be decided by a jury of not less than 3 or more than 12 men, who are to be men of honor and intelligence, and who are not members of any church, but believe the Bible and respect religion; men of the legal profession preferred. Disputed meaning of words decided by Webster's Dictionary and Smith's Bible Dictionary.

A DREAM.

I will now close with a dream that I had three nights ago and its interpretation. I thought the moon had fallen to the earth near where I was. I examined it and found that it had been so much decayed by age that its brilliancy had departed and was corroded so much that it was impossible to repair it; so I made a new one, when an intelligent school teacher came along on her way to school and admired my new moon very much and desired me to show it to her pupils, which I did, and then sent it about its business. I last saw it in the sky when it looked like a new moon when we first see it, but was clear and bright.

INTERPRETATION.

As the moon gets its light from the sun and lights the earth at night, so the truth comes from God and enlightens the benighted world through the church. As the moon became old and decayed, so the truth delivered by Christ and the Apostles has been set aside and the churches are teaching for doctrine commandments of men. As it was impossible to repair the decayed moon, so it is impossible to get the 1,000 different churches to lay aside their multitude of creeds and come back to the teachings of Christ, for I have been trying it for four years and now see that the only way is to reflect the same light upon the world that the old moon did in its youth, that was Christ and the early church. The teacher represents the faithful minister who is glad to receive the whole truth and have it taught to his pupils or members. As the new moon does not give much light, so I have not been able to get the mystery of the Kingdom before much of the world. As the moon will grow until a full moon lights the whole night, so will the truth that God ordained me to teach fill the earth. As the mellow light of the full moon fades away before the glowing light of the morning sun, even so will the light of my moon be swallowed up in the glorious brilliancy of the dawning of the day of the Son of Righteousness. Even so Lord may it be. Amen.

SEVENTH STEP.

The Kingdom of God—Thy Kingdom Come.—Mat. 6, 10.

No Gospel truth is so important as the Kingdom of God; yet no truth is less understood. In the Lord's Prayer it was the first subject in the petition, being before even our daily bread or the forgiveness of our sins; yet if you asked the Doctors of Divinity of this country what it was and how it was to be obtained, you would get a multitude of answers, none of which would be correct. I attended last August, at Cornwall, a conference of the Brotherhood of the Kingdom (so called) and obtained a lot of literature on the subject, none of which would direct the student hardly one step on the way to possess it. Yet many important truths were dropped there. One of the best was from Archdeacon Wood, D. D., in his valuable paper he said the Tree of Suffering is the tree of life; but did not tell us how we could obtain it by suffering.

What is the Kingdom of God?

In answering this question it is necessary to explain what a kingdom is. It is a people governed by a king, and may be either absolute as to have the governing power vested in one person, who's word is law; or it may be limited in which others are associated with the king, each of which have a power to assist in the governing power. The Kingdom of God or Christ, which means the same, will be like the latter; for in Rev. 3, 22: "To him that overcometh will I grant to sit with me in my throne, even as I overcome and am set down with my Father in His throne." These shall reign with Christ a thousand years, as we read in Revelation 2: 4, as that is the extent of Christ's reign on earth.

To describe the glory of this would be simply to describe the indescribable; language is inadequate. Could you find language to describe the beauty of the rose or lily to one that has never seen the light, what can I use to compare it with when beginnings of its equal is not on earth? Under the law it was said: "Eye hath not seen, nor ear heard, neither hath it entered into the heart of man the things that God hath prepared for them that love Him. Paul quotes this and adds in contrast in I Cor. 2: "But God hath revealed them to us by his spirit, for the spirit searches all things, yea the deep things of God." But any one who will seek it can, while on earth, realize its glory and beauty, which is very far ahead of the glory of Solomon's. Some teach that all who are saved will reign with Christ, but fail to tell who they will reign over; as a kingdom without subjects would not be worth possessing and would be like Alexander Selkirk's, who was wrecked on an uninhabited island. The poet makes him say:

    I am monarch of all I survey;
      To my right there is none to dispute;
    From the center all round to the sea,
      I'm the Lord of the foul and the brute.

His glory is described as follows:
    O Solitude where is the charms
      That sages have seen in thy face;
    Better dwell in the midst of alarm,
      Than to range in this horrible place.
    Society, friendship and love,
      Devinety bestowed upon man;
    O, had I the wings of a dove,
      How soon would I taste you again.

The term children of the kingdom refers to those who will reign, and not to the subjects; so who are they? Some say they are the lost sinners who inhabit through eternity that warm climate, which I think few would care to inhabit, even to be its ruler. Besides his impship might object to deviding his kingdom. Rev. 20:5, says: "The rest (wicked dead) lived not again until the thousand years were finshed." Others say their rule is to arrange the punishment of the sinners who sleep in their grave while God the judge has reserved the judgment to himself.

When Adam was created God could not give him a kingdom, for there were no subjects; so he done the best he could and gave the same kind that Alexander Selkirk had dominion over, the fowl and the brute; and if he had not transgressed Christ would not have had a kingdom. But God never made a mistake and knew what he, as well as the serpent, would do when He created them, and if he had known the mystery of God, he could have got back in Paradise, or God's dwelling place, which means the same as the kingdom, but God purposely hid the way to repair the broken law for 4,000 years, so that Christ might reveal it when he came and have subjects as well as kings. For that reason he gave them the law of burnt offerings and priestly service so that those that obeyed it might dwell upon the earth and be subjects and go back to the law of sacrifices during the time that Christ and his 144,000 kings should reign over them in the Golden City, the New Jerusalem that shall come down to the renewed earth which the subjects will not be permitted to enter, as described in Revelations 21. John says: "I saw a new heaven and a new earth, for the first heaven and the first earth were passed away and there was no more sea. And I, John, saw the holy city, New Jerusalem, coming down from God out of heaven prepared as a bride adorned for her husband. And I heard a great voice out of heaven saying, 'Behold the tabernacle of God is with men and He will dwell with them and they shall be His and God Himself shall be with them and be their God.'" Those who received the mystery while it was preached will raise in the first resurrection, which will take place as soon as enough more receive the seal after it is preached or published to the world to complete the 144,000; and with them now living who accept the truth will be caught up to meet the Lord in the air, and so be forever with the Lord as explained in Thessalonians 4: 18. This will take place three and one-half years before the end of the age. During that time there will be the great tribulation, which will last to the end, when the world will be burned with so great heat that the rocks and stones will be reduced to the finest dust and the sea will be dried and the mountains will be cast in it and the world will become a vast plain; and all of the righteous dead who have lived since Adam will be raised and dwell upon it and Christ and his kings shall reign over them; and the christians who have lived since the mystery was wrested from the church will be among the subjects. Satan will be chained during the thousand years and the people will come once a year to the earthly Jerusalem to offer their sacrifices, but not in the heavenly, which Paul says is free while the earthly is in bondage with her children. Gal. 4: 25-26.

The truths of the kingdom few will accept when they hear it, for they will be wedded to their churches and will try to believe that they are right, but when the 144,000, as described in Rev. 14: 1-6, are caught up, will abandon their churches and come to the Apostolic. But it will be too late to be crowned, but will dwell in the holy city and be servants and serve Christ and his brethren day and night. Rev. 7: 14-16. They will be a number that no man can number coming from every nation, while the

144,000 will come from the eleven tribes of Israel, for Dan is excluded for the Antechrist will come from his tribe.

When will the kingdom come is the next question. It will come just 6,000 years after creation, for as God was 6 days creating all things, and a thousand years is as one day, and the seventh day was the Sabbath. So the seventh thousand years will be the millenial Sabbath. This was the unanimous opinion of the early church. I will give an extract from the 15th chapter of the Epistle of Barnabas: "The Sabbath is mentioned at the beginning of creation, thus the Lord made in six days the works of his hands and made an end on the seventh day, and rested on it and sanctified it." This implies that the Lord will finish all things in 6,000 years, for a day with Him is a thousand years. Therefore, my children, in six days, that is in six thousand years, all things will be finished, and be rested on the seventh day. This means when His son cometh again He shall destroy the time of the wicked man and judge the ungodly and change the sun and the moon and the stars. Then shall He truely rest on the seventh day. Moreover, He says thou shall sanctify it with pure hands and a pure heart. If any one can sanctify the day which God has sanctified, except he is pure in heart and in all thing, we are deceived. One properly resting sanctifies it when we have received the promise; wickedness no longer existing and all things having been made new by the Lord, shall be able to work righteousness. Then we shall be able to sanctify it, having first been sanctified ourselves. Further He says your new moons and your Sabbaths I cannot endure. Ye perceive how He speaks; your present Sabbaths are not acceptable to me. When giving rest to all things I shall make a beginning of the eighth day. This is the beginning of another world. Therefore we keep the eighth day with joyfulness;

"the day also that Jesus raised from the dead." So we keep the eighth day, or the first day of the second week, in honor of the beginning of God's eternal reign, which will be at the end of the millennium, when Christ shall return the government to the Father. We discover here the mistake that is made in calling the first day of the week the Sabbath, as that only applies to the day we call the seventh, or Saturday, and no where did the early church call it the Sabbath, for that means seventh. Some say the day was changed, but that is not so, for no one has any right to change any of God's ordinances. The Catholic church claims the honor, but are not any more entitled to it than they are of the honor of abolishing sacrifices; for God said in Isaiah 1: 11, "I delight not in the blood of bullocks, or lambs, or he goats," and in verse 13, "Bring no more vain oblations; incense is an abomination unto Me; the new moons and Sabbaths, the callings of assemblies I cannot sway with; it is iniquity, even the solemn meetings." So the Sabbath was not changed but put away. The Jews were taught to hold it in honor of the millennium when they were taught that Christ would be their king and reign over them. But we are told we shall be equal to him and reign with him, so to worship the day would be a sort of self-worship. The first day is not a day of rest, but a day of good things; a day of rejoicing and of gift giving; not a day to make money, but a day of charity and giving of thanks. The fathers taught that we were not to kneel in prayer, but to pray standing with uplifted hands, and if we fasted on that day we were guilty of the body and blood of Christ.

THE GROWTH OF THE KINGDOM.

Some think that the best thing before us is Christ's reign; but it is far behind what is to follow. God has planted in our hearts a desire and hope of something better ahead, for He says: " Of the increase of His government there will be no end." The good is put aside to give place to the better, as the Sabbath was put away to give place for the Lord's day.

SEEK THE BEST PLACE IN THE KINGDOM.

There will be as many grades of honor in Christ's kingdom as there is grades of offices in this government, from the president down to the trustee of the district school. Paul says in I Cor. 15: 41: "There is one glory of the sun and another glory of the moon, and another glory of the stars, for one star differeth from another star in glory. So also is the resurrection of the dead." We find the best places in the kingdom are filled by the four beasts or living creatures, as in the revised version in Revelations 4, who are in the midst of and round about the throne. The first of these will be filled by Peter, who, as Tertulien tells us unbored the kingdom; and the next by John, who was first to enter in; and the other two will be filled by the first two who reopens the kingdom by discovering the mystery and publishing it.

Twelve of the thrones of the twenty-four elders will be filled by twelve of the fourteen Apostles (as Paul and Barnabas were added), and the other twelve thrones will be filled by the first twelve who accepts the truth taught by the last two beasts, who will assist them in their great work of revealing to the world the Mystery of God.

Covet earnestly the best places, for he who will be first to pay the price will get it.

Tell me how far we are from the end of 6,000 year from creation and I will tell you how far we are from the Lord's second advent. We are not wholely without chronological records, as we have what claims to be one in our reference Bibles which places creation

4,004 years before Christ, and we have 1899 on our calander since, making 5,903. The author of these dates was not inspired and might have made a mistake. Let us see. Saul was anointed king 1095 years before Christ, which appears to be correct (see margin 1 Samuel, 10). Now turn to Joshua 18, and we have the account of deviding the land and date 1444. Divide and we have 349 years. Acts 13, 19, the inspired writer says: "He devided the land by lot and after that he gave unto them judges about the space of 450." Here we see a mistake of 100 years, which added makes the 6,000; but this is not exactly correct, as the end is not less than 7 years ahead, which I will explain later.

EIGHTH STEP.

Antechrist.

"I am come in my Father's name and ye receive me not; if another shall come in his own name him ye will receive." John 5: 43.

God created all things in six days and made an end. Before he made man he made the angels. The number, John tells us, were equal to the children of men that should come into the world. It is a comforting thought that we each have our angel as a body guard and servant. As men differ in strength, ability, influence and power, so do the angels, and each have their respective duties.

The one first called the serpent He gave the earth as his dominion. Christ calls him the prince of this world, and he exhibits more power over its governments than men give him credit for, as there is but two influences in the world, good and evil, and he is author of all the evil, as since his fall he has exerted all of his power to defeat God's plans and bring all men to a level with himself. He is omnipresent and has a host of fallen angels to aid him in his efforts, but often overreaches in his zeal, as he did at Christ's crucifixion. His personal presence is before the throne now where he is ever accusing the saints to God, as we read in Revelations 12: 10, and Job 1: 6-12. In the former we read that the dragon or serpent called satan and the devil is cast out of heaven and his angels with him. This will take place three and a half years before the end of the age, when he will set up his kingdom upon the earth and rule it through the great tribulation; for we read: "Woe to the inhabitants of the earth and the sea, for the devil has come down to you having great wrath, because he knoweth that he hath but a short time."

As Christ can put his spirit in men who are willing to receive it, so can satan, and his reign as antechrist will be through the body of some man who the world will see as a political ruler, and as men have loved to serve him in the past they will get their fill during this season; but those who have excepted the truth and received the kingdom will escape, for they will be caught up alive about the time satan descends. Christ saw the vision of satan descending like lightning and said: "Watch ye, therefore, and pray always that ye may be accounted worthy to escape these things that shall come to pass and stand before the Son of Man," Luke 21: 26; and, "because thou hast kept the words of my patients I also will keep thee from the hour of temptation that shall come upon all the world to try them that dwell on the earth," Rev. 3: 10. There has been much speculation as to who he will be, but it will not matter much as we know whose spirit he will have and he will be an Israelite of the tribe of Dan, and for that reason Dan was not among the 144,000 that were seated as recorded in the 7th of Revelations, and in Geneses 4. 4-17: "Dan shall be a serpent by the way, an adder in the path that bitteth the horses heels so that his rider shall fall backward. Dan shall judge his people as one of the tribes of Israel."

The early "Fathers" sustain this, as I will show by quotations from Hippolyters, Bishop of Partus, who lived and wrote in the second century: "Thus did the Scriptures teach beforetime of this lion and lion's whelp. And in like manner also was it written regarding Antechrist. For Moses speaks thus: "Dan is a lion's whelp, and he shall leap from Bashon." But that no one may err by supposing that this is said of Christ, let him attend carrefully to the matter. Dan he says is a lion's whelp, and in naming the tribe of Dan, and that the case stands thus; we see also from the words of Jacob: " Let Dan be a serpent, lying upon the ground, biting the horses heel." What then is meant by the serpent, but Antechrist, the deceiver, who deceived Eve and supplanted Adam. But since it is necessary to prove this assertion by sufficient testimony, we shall not shrink from the task. Out of the tribe of Dan then that tyrant and king, that dread judge, that son of the devil is destined to spring and arise; the prophet testifies when he says Dan shall judge his people as one tribe of Israel. But some one may say that this refers to Samson, who sprang from the tribe of Dan and judged the people 20 years. Well, the prophecy had its partial fulfillment in Samson, but its complete fulfillment is reserved for Antechrist; for Jeremiah also speaks of this effect. From Dan we are to hear the sound of the surging of his horses; the whole land trembled at the sound of the neighing of the driving of his horses. Another prophet says: " He shall gather all of his strength from the east, even to the west." The same Hippolytus says of him: " In his first step he will be gentle, loving, quiet, pious, pacific, hating iniquity, detesting gifts, not allowing idolatry, loving the scriptures, reverencing priests, honoring his elders, detesting adultery, giving no heed to slander, not admitting oaths, kind to strangers and the poor, compassionate." And then he will work wonders, cleansing lepers, raising paralytics, expelling demons, raising the dead, helping widows, defending orphans, loving all, reconciling in love those who contend, and saying to such, let not the son go down on your wrath, and he will not require gold, nor love silver, nor seek riches. And all this will he do corruptly and deceitfully, and with the purpose of deluding all to make him king, for if it were possible he would deceive the very elect. When they see such great power and virtue in him they will meet to make him king. Who will say: We will confide in thee, and acknowledge thee to be just upon the whole earth; we hope to be saved by three, and by thy mouth we have received just and incorruptable judgment. And at first that deceitful and lawless one will refuse such glory; but the men persisting and holding up him will declare him king. And therefore he will be lifted up in heart, and he who was formerly gentle, will become violent, and he who persued love will become pitiless, and the humble in heart will become haughty and inhuman, and the hater of unrighteousness will persecute the righteous. Then when he is elevated to his kingdom he will marshall war and in his wrath he will smite three mighty kings, and after that he will rebuild the temple of Jerusalem and restore it speedily and give it over to the Jews. And then he will be lifted up in heart against every man; yea, he will speak blasphemy against God, thinking in his deceit that he will be king upon the earth forever, not knowing (miserable wretch) that his kingdom is soon to be brought to naught and that he will quickly have to meet the fire prepared for him along with all who trust in him. For Daniel said: "I will make my covenant for one week." He indicated seven years, and the half of the week is for the preaching of the prophets, and the other half of the week, that is to say, three and a half years, Antechrist will reign upon the earth, and after this his kingdom and glory will be taken away.

Again he says, "The heavens will not give their dew, the clouds will not give the rain, the earth will refuse to yield its fruit, the sea will be filled with stench, the rivers will be dried up, the fish of the sea shall die, men shall perish with hunger and thirst; the father embracing son, the mother embracing daughter, will die together, and there will be none to bury them; for the whole earth will be filled with the odor arising from their dead bodies; and the sea not receiving the flood of the rivers will become like mire and will be filled with an unlimited stench. Then there will be a mighty pestilence upon the whole earth, and then, too, inconsolable lamentation and measureless weeping. Then men will deem them happy who are dead before them, and will say to them, "open your sepulchers and take us miserable beings in; open your receptacles for the reception of your wretched kinsmen and acquaintances. Happy are ye in that ye have not seen our day. Happy are ye in that ye have not had to witness this painful life of ours." Then that abominable one will send his command throughout every government, saying, "A mighty king has risen upon the earth; come ye all and worship him; come and see the strength of his kingdom; for behold he will give you corn and he will bestow on you wine and great riches and lofty honors, for the whole earth and sea obey his command and by reason of the scarcity of food all will go to him and worship him. And he will put his mark on their right hand and upon their forehead, so that no one can put the honorable mark of the cross on their forehead by their right hand, but his hand is bound. When men have received his seal, and find neither food or water, they will reproach him with a voice of anguish, saying, give us to eat and drink, for we all faint with hunger and all manner of straits, and bid the heavens yield us water and drive off the beasts that devour us. Then will the crafty one answer, mocking them. The heavens refuse to give rain, the earth yields not again her fruit, whence then can I give you food? Then on hearing the words of this deceiver, these miserable men will perceive that this is the wicked accuser, and will mourn in anguish, and weep vehemently, and beat their face with their hands, and tear their hair, and lacerate their cheeks with their nails, while they say to each other: Woe for the calamity! Woe for the deceitful contract! Woe for the deceitful covenant! Woe for the mighty mischance! How have we been beguiled by the deceiver! How have we been joined to him! How have we been caught in his toils! How have we been taken in his abominable net! How have we heard the scriptures and understood them not! For truly those who are engrossed with the affairs of life and with the lusts of this world will be easily brought over to the accuser then and sealed by him."

I will now turn from this wonderful description given by Hippolytus, although I have not quoted half of his "discourse on the end of the world and on Antechrist and on the second coming of our Lord." I first thought he was wrong by saying he would be burned after the three years and a half, but he referred to the son of Dan, who would so sell himself to the Devil; for he could not do it and be guiltless, for it would be better for him if he had never been born. As God dwells in his children, so the serpent, who tries to imitate God in all things, dwells in his to add to their misery. So the Antechrist is both the serpent and the son of him. While the latter goes to perdition, the former is to be chained in the abyss for a thousand years, after which God has more use for him, for those who are subjects in Christ's kingdom are, after the millenium, to be subjected to another temptation and tribulation, under which most of those who were formerly saved will fall, as they are a camp compared to a multitude as numerous as the sands of the sea. See Rev. 20: 7-10. But those who reign with Christ and receive His kingdom will not be subject to this second temptation, for they will be beyond satan's power and shall reign with Christ for ever and ever.

Do not think Hippolytus has overdrawn the picture of the great tribulation and Antechrist, for he has not told the half. The Bible is filled with descriptions. Christ said if these days were not shortened no flesh could be saved. Paul said, 2 Thes. 2: 8-12, " Then shall that wicked be revealed whom the Lord shall consume with the spirit of his mouth and shall destroy with the brightness of his coming: whose coming is after the working of Satan with all power and signs, and living wonders, and will all deceivableness of unrighteousness in them that perish; because they received not the love of the truth that they might be saved. And for this cause God shall send them strong delusions that they should believe a lie; that they all might be damned who believe not the truth, but have pleasure in unrighteousness." Daniel in latter part of chapters 8 and 11 describes him and tells of his wonderful power and says he will gain his kingdom by flattery. Also in Revelations 18: 11, he is described as a " beast coming up out of the earth and he had two horns like a lamb and he spake like a dragon, and he exercised all of the power of the first beast before him and caused the earth and them that dwell therein to worship the first beast, whose deadly wound was healed. And he doth great wonders so that he maketh fire come down from heaven on the earth in the sight of men and deceiveth them that dwell on the earth by the means of these miracles which he hath power to do in the sight of the beast, saying to them that dwell on the earth that they should make an image of the beast which had the wound by the sword and did live. And he had power to give life unto the image of the beast, that the image of the beast should speak and cause that as many as would not worship the image of the beast should be killed. And he called all both great and small, rich and poor, free and bound, to receive a mark in their right hand, or in their forehead; and that no man might buy or sell save he that had the mark or the name of the beast or the number of his name. Here is wisdom. Let him that hath understanding count the number of the beast, for it is the number of a man, and his number is six hundred threescore and six.

Hippolytus says the numerical letters in 666 make the words "I deny," and says, "In the time of that hater of all good will be the seal, the tenor of which will be this: I deny the maker of heaven and earth; I deny the baptism; I deny my former service, and attach myself to thee and I believe in thee." In Isaiah 14: 12, "How art thou fallen from heaven, O Lucifer, son of the morning; how art thou cut down to the ground, which did weaken the nations! for thou hast said in thine heart, I will ascend into heaven, I will exalt my throne above the stars of God; I will sit also upon the mount of the congregation, in the side of the north; I will ascend above the heights of the clouds; I will be like the Most High. Yet thou shalt be brought down to hell, to the shades of the pit. They that see thee shall narrowly look upon thee, and consider thee, saying: Is this the man that made the earth to tremble and did shake kingdoms; that made the world as a wilderness and destroyed the cities thereof; that opened not the house of his prisoners. All the kings of the nation, even also of them, be in glory everyone in his own house. But thou are cast out of thy grave like an abominable branch, and as the remnant of them that are slain, thrust through with a sword, and go down to the stones of the pit as a carcas trodden under foot. Thou shalt not be joined with them in burial because thou has destroyed thy land and slain thy people. The seed of evil doers shall never be renowned."

Five years ago I attended the meetings of the great

Brooklyn revival, also some meetings at Simpson's Tabernacle, 690 Eight Evenue, New York, and attended one of his lectures to his class of missionary students. He expounded (or pretended to) the eighth chapter of Daniel. He said he could not accept the doctrine of a personal Antechrist, for he believed the scriptures applied to him were fulfilled in the line of the Popes, and the $3\frac{1}{2}$ years, and 42 months time, and half a time, and 1260 days, all of which mean the same time, or $3\frac{1}{2}$ years, as the Roman year had but 360 days, or 12 months of 30 days each, and after the calendar got too far behind the sun three months were added to allow the calendar to catch up to the sun. I would like to ask him which of the Popes exalted his throne above God's, or blasphemed God, or sat in the temple at Jerusalem, or caused an image to speak, or called down fire from heaven in the presence of men. I consider it very dangerous doctrine to teach, for make a man believe there is no personal Antechrist and he will accept him as Christ when he comes, and accept his seal. I had a vision and was in Antechrist's kingdom, a day or so after this, and saw men who refused to accept him sent off to the slaughter, and them that did were dressed in uniform consisting of a cloak of gay colors and cape and turban cap, all of gay color and heavy fringe, and among those thus dresssed I saw one of Simpson's leading workers, who blindly followed him.

As to who the Antechrist will be I do not pretend to say, but a passage in Revelation points to a Bonaparte, for which says the eighth earthly ruler, which is Antechrist, will be of the seventh, which was Napoleon. Again the Greek numerical letters in Bonaparte 666. Prophetic scholars pointed to Jerome, who died in 1891, but left two sons. After the Bonapartes were expelled from France, Jerome took the oath of allegiance to the French Republic, but afterwards reconsidered it, not on his own account, but he had visions of empire for his son. Victor, one son, is an officer in the Russian army, and is very popular with the Czar. I read that he lately sent him a telegram hoping the time was not far distant when he would be reinstated on his throne, and that he had as many friends in France as there are in Russia. I recently read of a book published last winter and suppressed, that stated that the army was opposed to the government and a majority desired to restore the monarchy. It will do to watch him.

NINTH STEP.

The Two Witnesses.

And at that time shall Michael stand up, that great prince which standeth for the children of thy people: and there shall be a time of trouble such as never was since there was a nation, even to that same time: and at that time thy people shall be delivered every one that shall be found written in the book. Daniel 12: 1.

No men in the world's history are to fill as important a position for good as the last great prophets. There is nearly as much prophecy concerning them in the old testament as there is of our Seviour. As Christ is referred to under many different names, so are they. In many places only one is referred to, as in the text where he is called Michael, the great prince, which proves he or they will come from the tribe of Judah and of the line of David. In Zach. 4: 6, he is called Zerubbabel, which is you see the Bible dictionary of proper names, mean prince of Judah; and the olive branches, or trees, as they are called in Revelations 11: 4, where in both places they are called the two candlesticks. And in Isaiah 11: 1, we find more proof he is a descendant of Jesse, David's father. To compare Isaiah 11 with Revelations 11, you will see they refer to the same person. One says, " He shall smite the earth with the rod of his mouth, and with the breath of his lips shall he slay the wicked, and righteousness shall be the girdle of his loins, and faithfulness shall be the girdle of his reign." The other, " I will give power to my two witnesses, and they shall prophecy one thousand two hundred and threescore days, clothed in sackcloth. These are the two olive trees and the two candlesticks which stand before the God of the earth, and if any man will hurt them, fire proceedeth out of their mouth and devoureth their enemies, and if any man hurt them, he must in this manner be killed. These have power to shut heaven that it rain not in the days of their prophecy (or in $3\frac{1}{2}$ years), and have power over waters to turn them to blood and to smite the earth with all plagues as often as they will. And after they shall have finished their testimony, the beast that ascended out of the bottomless pit shall make war against them and shall overcome them and kill them. And their dead bodies shall lie in the street, this is spiritually called Soddom and Egypt, where also our Lord was crucified. (It is Jerusalem called Soddom, or the land of sin, because Antechrist will then have his throne there.) And they of the people and tongues and nations shall see their dead bodies three days and a half and shall not suffer their dead bodies to be put in graves. And they that dwell upon the earth shall rejoice over them and make merry, and shall send gifts one to another, because these two prophets tormented them that dwelt on the earth. And after three days and a half the spirit of life from God entered into them and they stood upon their feet, and great fear fell on them that saw them. And they heard a great voice from heaven saying unto them, come up hither. And they ascended up to heaven in a cloud and their enemies beheld them. And the same hour there was a great earthquake and a tenth part of the city fell, and in the earthquake were slain of men, seven thousand men. The second woe is past and behold the third woe cometh quickly. And the seventh angel sounded; and there were great voices in heaven saying the kingdoms of this world are become the kingdoms of our Lord and of his Christ, and he shall reign for ever and ever."

Here we have a pretty full history of the two witnesses. As God saves the best things for the last, so he has saved the greatest of the prophets for the last. And in them the power of all the former prophets are combined. Moses and Aaron are a good type of them, and as Moses was the principle law giver and leader of them, so will it be with these. The one called in Malachi 4: 5. Elijah will be the principle one and leader, while the other will receive the truth from him and act the part of a priest or spokesman, as Aaron was to Moses, and assist him in publishing the mystery of the kingdom, or the seal by which the saints will be sealed to the world, as one of the early fathers tell us. Malachi says, " I will send you Elijah the prophet before the coming of the great and dreadful day of the Lord. And he shall turn the hearts of the fathers to the children, and the hearts of the children to their fathers, lest I come and smite the earth with a curse." This is not of course to be taken literally, for Christ said, " I came to turn the father against the son, and son against the father," but he meant by the fathers, the Apostles, or fathers of the early church, and by the sons he means us. If apostolic faith and power had not been lost there would be nothing to restore, and no need for Elijah to come, for his mission first is to restore to the church the gospel in its apostolic purity. And if all men would receive the truth taught by him there would be no Antechrist to come, for he would be converted and no need of the curse, but as the masses will not receive the truth, the curse, or great tribulation, and Antechrist will have to come. So the first duty of the witnesses is to give the seal to all who will receive it, but no church as a whole will receive it, for he came not to save the nominal church but to take a people out of the churches, and to get the remainder of the 144,000 will take three and a half years, for part of them were sealed before the seal was lost, or during the first three hundred years of the Christian era. Rev. 7: 2, says, "I saw another angel ascend from the East having the seal of the living God, and he cried with a loud voice to the four angels to whom it was given to hurt the earth and the sea, saying, hurt not the earth, neither the sea, nor the trees, till we have sealed the servants of God in their foreheads, and I heard the number of them that were sealed, and there sealed 144,000 of all the tribes of the children of Israel (except Dan)." By not hurting the earth or trees means in this period there will be no insects or pests to prevent the bountiful product of the earth, so it would yield enough to last during the $3\frac{1}{2}$ years of famine, but in war it will be wasted as it was when Titus took Jerusalem, and it will be the duty of the witnesses to collect and store for the christians provisions for the famine, for God will cause them to collect in some place in this country where Antechrist cannot enter, for in Rev. 12, the church is represented as the woman and the 144,000 as the child. "And she brought forth a man child who was to rule all nations with a rod of iron, and the child was caught up to God and to his throne. And the woman fled into the wilderness where she had a place prepared of God that they should feed her there a thousand two hundred and threescore days (or $3\frac{1}{2}$ years)."

The christians that understand these things and have property, will sell it and bring their money to the witnesses and have all things common as the early christians did, and the abundance of grain will make it very cheap, for it will be of little use to hoard property when we expect to be translated into heaven in three years or less, and those who do not and have farms will not be of any value through the famine and they will be burned up with the world at the end of the age. And money even to the antichristians will not be of any value to them during the tribulation, for it will not buy food when there is none, and those that have food will not exchange it for money, for Hippolytus says, "At that time silver and gold will be cast out into the streets and no one shall gather them, for all things shall be held an offense."

Some say that the prediction of the coming of Elijah was fulfilled in John the Baptist, and I was of that opinion until the Holy Spirit set me right. But a close study of the text will show that he did not fulfill the prophecy, for the great and dreadful day of the Lord is his second, nor first advent. He preached repentence but did not restore all things. He told the Jews, as recorded in John 1: 20-24, he was not Christ, nor Elijah, as prophecied in Malachi, but was the voice of one crying in the wilderness, make straight the way of the Lord, as saith the prophet Isaiah (40: 3). During His first advent the Jews and even the Disciples did not understand that Christ was to come the second time, and those that received Him supposed all prophecies concerning Him was to then be fulfilled, and the doubting Jews said he is not Christ, for Elijah has not come, and John said he was not him, and he was to come first. So Jesus did not attempt to explain to them his second advent, but said if Elijah is in the way of your accepting Me, accept John as Elijah, whom you slew, and you cannot deny me. Christ said in Matt. 11: 14, "If ye will receive it this is Elijah that was for to come." As a forerunner of Christ and a preparer of the way, John and the witnesses fill the same place, are entitled to the same name, but nowhere in the old testament can I see any prediction that was fulfilled in John. The one in Isaiah 40, applies to the witnesses, for it says, "Prepare ye the way of the

Lord; make straight in the desert a highway for our God. Every valley shall be exalted and every mountain and hill shall be made low, and the crooked shall be made straight and the rough places plain, and the glory of the Lord shall be revealed and all flesh shall see it together, for the mouth of the Lord hath spoken it." This was not fulfilled in John's day, but will be at the end, when the earth will be burned by the command of the raised and flying witnesses, when the rocks will melt and be reduced to dust, and mountains and hills be moved in the seas and valleys, and the earth will be as white as snow, like a bride prepared for her husband, as the hidden word of the Apostle John declares, "The witnesses will not come from the people now known as Jews, but from the descendants of those who were converted to Christ by the preaching of the Apostles and forsook their Jewish faith and customs and became identified with the Christians and lost their identity as Jews." Perhaps 50,000 Jews were converted during the first century. I find a chronological list in which I saw that the Apostles James, John and James the less were cousins of the Lord and decendants of David, as well as several other prominent New Testament characters. Judge and James, the just bishop of Jerusalem, were the Lord's brothers. None of the early Fathers admitted that the coming of Elijah was fulfilled by John the Baptist. Hippolytus refers to him three time and calls him one of the witnesses who is to occupy half of the last seven years.

In the instructions of Commodianus, 240 A. D., "Nero (Antechrist) shall be raised up from hell. Elijah shall first come to seal the beloved ones. at which time the whole earth on all sides, for seven years shall tremble. But Elijah shall occupy half of the time and Nero shall occupy half. Then the whole Babylon (Rome) being reduced to ashes, its embers shall thence be advanced to Jerusalem and the Latin conqueror shall then say, I am Christ whom ye always pray to. He does many wonders, since he is the false prophet. Asterius Urbanus, 232 A. D., "And I saw another angel ascending from the east having the seal of the living God." He speaks of Elijah, the prophet, who is the predecessor of Antechrist for the restoration of the church from the great and intolerable persecution.

The Jew in his argument with Justin, the martyr, says Jesus was not the Christ, for Elijah was to come first. Justin explains that there was to be two advents and the coming of Elijah was to preced the second. Tertulien only refers to Elijah once in his writings that has come down to us, and that is on the resurrection, to refute the belief that the resurrection was already past by referring to future events that must occur before the resurrection. Up to the present moment they have not tribe by tribe smitten their breasts looking on Him whom they pierced. No one as yet has fallen in with Elijah. No one has as yet escaped from Antechrist. No one has as yet had to bewail the downfall of Babylon (Rome). And is there now anybody who has risen again except the heretics?

Some of the Fathers seemed to convey the opinion that the Elijah to come was the same one that walked the earth twenty-five hundred years ago, or rather ran it when a weak woman got after him, and hid himself where none but God could find him and rebuked him by saying, "What doest thou here Elijah?" For he said, "It is enough now, O Lord, take away my life for there is a woman after me." He was no slouch of a runner for he outran the king's chariot horses when there was a thunder shower after him. I am not in the habit of getting prophets by the ears, but he needed a gentle rebuke for making fun at Baal's poor, or rather fat prophets, who had been so well fed at the Queen's table, by telling them to cry louder, for their God was on a journey or asleep and needed waking, when they were doing their best.

What a relief it must have been to Ahab to have 400 of his complimentary guests drop out of his board at one time. But I think that the Lord will require some one of a little more courage to beard the great wild beast in his den. After all he was well noted for his courage as for his timidity. Few men would care to face the man that had been seeking his life for three years, or face and put to death 400 of Baal's prophets, or none but Antechrist would think of looking where he did for a match to light his fire after he had prepared his liquid kindling wood. He was a great prophet and did his work faithfully, and the Lord overlooked his weakness and sent his chariot and fiery chargers and took him home in great style, and there he will let him rest, for the Lord is not so short of material that he has got to use a man twice over. Why any man can be Elijah if he will get the same spirit and power! It is easy enough if he dares to be a Daniel. But they are hard to find for I have vainly looked five years for one. All that I have found will not stand alone without being propped up.

Rev. Mr. Rauscenbusche, of New York, read before the Brotherhood meeting last August, a paper entitled "The Coming Apostle," which showed the deep spirituality of the writer. As near as I can recollect, in part he said, "He would lay aside all creeds and churchism, would receive and walk in the Holy Spirit, be ignored and rejected by his former friends, churches and relatives; persecuted by the churches and christians; would be a bearer of the cross until the cross bore him; would be wafted on the pinions of angels to his future home, where he would be received with songs of triumph." Any who would like to fill the bill hold up your hand, for there are places waiting for a number of such.

The end of the age will occur on Passover week, which I believe is in April, and if the names of the two witnesses are published by next April, all may know that the end will occur in April, 1907, and the rupture or first resurrection in the autumn of 1903. But if those who reject these teachings it will come to like a thief in the night. "But ye," says the Apostles, "are not of the night." Those who have set the time of the end have not closely studied the scriptures and ignored the reign of Antechrist and of the witnesses. Some who have closely studied prophecy have placed the time early in 1900. Among those was the saintly Edward Irving, who lived in England 65 years ago and was ejected from the church of England because he was too pious to suit the great worldly church, but most of his congregation stuck to him.

I have not exhausted the predictions of the witnesses in the bible. I heard the evangelist, G. C. Needham, in his sermon on angels truly say that the angels of the seven churches in Revelations second and third were men. They are types of the history of the church through the ages and we are living in the two last. The angel of Philadelphia can be no one but he who will give the key or seal to the 144,000 who will escape the tribulation. "These things saith he that hath the key of David, he that openeth and no man shutteth, and shutteth and no man openeth (that means the same as, who thou shalt bind on earth shall be bound in heaven, and who thou shalt loose on earth shall be loosed in heaven, as He said to Peter, for as Peter opened the Kingdom Elijah will reopen it). Behold, I set before thee an open door and no man can shut it (as the Nicaen council did before). Behold, I will make them which say they are Jews (Christians) and are not and do lie. Behold,

I will make them come and worship before thy feet and to know that I have loved thee. Because thou hast kept the words of my patients I also will keep thee from the hour of temptation (tribulation) that shall come upon all the world to try them that dwell upon the earth. Behold, I come quickly; hold that fast which thou hast that no man take thy crown. Him that overcometh will I make a pillar in the temple of my God, and he shall go no more out."

The angel of the church of Laodecea, called the Amen (the last prophet), the faithful and true witness (one of the witnesses), the beginning of the creation of God (one who will restore the truth and bring in the kingdom), is the same as the one of Philadelphia, and those who accept his message will leave Laodecea and join the former, while the latter is the popular or lukewarm churches of to-day which will have to pass through the tribulation. The angel's message is " I know thy works that thou are neither cold nor hot. I would that thou wert cold or hot. Because thou art lukewarm and neither cold nor hot I will spew thee out of my mouth. Because thou sayest I am rich and increased in goods and have need of nothing and knoweth not that thou are wretched and miserable and poor and blind and naked, I counsel thee to buy of me gold tried in the fire, that thou mayest be rich, and white raiment that thou mayest be clothed and the shame of thy nakedness do not appear, and anoint thine eyes with eyesalve that thou mayest see. As many as I love I rebuke and chasten. Be zealous therefore and repent. Behold, I stand at the door and knock; if any man hear my voice and will open the door I will come in to him and sup with him and he with me. To him that overcometh will I grant to sit with me in my throne even as I also overcome and am set down with my father in his throne."

Who and where are the witnesses? Look among

the great theologians, but not many of the mighty are chosen. There was one, Nicodemus, among the doctors of the law, in Christ's time, and he was afraid of the light but was anxious to secretly learn the truth. There may be one now but I have not found him. I have said that I would rather undertake the task of bringing Robert G. Ingersoll into the kingdom than a D. D., for I believe he was honest and would accept a gospel founded on common sense and reason. I do not wonder that the world is full of infidelity when they try to cram down our throats such nonsense as Imputed Righteousness and the snake story. As no prophet is honored in his own country, we need not look among them that have received honors from men. As they will be dressed in sackcloth there is no need of looking among them that wear broadcloth and steam laundried linen and visit a barbershop thrice a week. You will have no trouble to find men who claim to be them; I know of four or five. When you find a man who is dispised for his piety, and can explain how Peter earned the keys of the kingdom, and what the Mystery of God that was hid from all ages and generations, as Paul says in Ephesians 3d, is and how the mystery became lost, and what the meaning of the Cross of Christ is, you may put your finger on him as the man; and the man that receives him in the name of a prophet and aids him in his work, will receive a prophet's reward. As Elijah's mantle fell on Elisha at his translation, so the mantle of the 144,000 will fall on the witnesses at the rapture after which they will have power. God says: "Behold, I make all things new." Before a man builds a new house he removes the old one. Then the Amen or Witness will show Antechrist that he has power over fire also, and when he takes his flight from the earth he says the word and the earth becomes a ball of fire. That is why he is the beginning of the creation of God. Commodianas says:

"Amen flames on the nations, suddenly there is darkness with the din of heaven. The Lord casts down His eyes so that the earth trembles. He cries out so all may hear: "Long have I been silent while I bore your doings.' They cry out together, complaining and groaning too late." They howl, they bewail, nor is there room found for the wicked. What shall the mother do for her sucking child when she herself is burned up? In flames of fire the Lord will judge the wicked. The flames will not touch the just. Such will be the heat that the stones themselves will melt. The wind assemble into lightning, the heavenly wrath rages and wherever the wicked man fleeth he is seized upon by the fire, as the hidden words of John declares." This is the only quotation or reference to John's other book of revelations, as it was hid then. Commodianas lived 200 years after Christ. There is a larger work of his on this subject that I have not seen.

TENTH STEP.

Baptism and Hobby Horses.

"Having our hearts sprinkled from an evil conscience and our bodies washed with pure water."—Heb. 10: 22.

Last winter I made a hobbyhorse; not for me to ride, for it would not be becoming nor profitable for me to spend my time jolting on a hobbyhorse, but for my little grandson; and a prouder little fellow you could rarely find than he was when he mounted his steed and started on his first ride. Nothing pleases a baby boy as well as a horse, and this to him completely filled the bill, for of course babies could not manage real live horses; but it is a horse to him. And we named it Dot, after a horse his father owned, and if you tell him it is not a horse he will say it is, for grandpa says it is and I guess grandpa knows what a horse is. If he falls or his mother spanks him, he goes to his horse and rides away all of the pain. I believe a hobbyhorse is a fine thing and I wish every little boy had one. The beauty of it is they take so little room; the little fellow will ride all day on a single yard of carpet. But we hope to soon see them outgrown and put away, for we would be sorry to see our grown up sons spending their time riding hobbyhorses and playing with children's toys and drawing milk from their mother's breast, when they ought to be managing a coach and four. I knew a man (if 50 years and 6 feet of growth will make one), who was sole heir to vast estates, that never outgrew his hobbyhorse and spent his time playing with children's toys, and his mind never developed enough to realize the value of money. Paul says, "When I was a child, I spoke as a child, I understood as a child, I thought as a child; but when I became a man I put away childish things."

Water baptism is simply a child's plaything, which we are to enjoy when we are first converted or are babes in Christ. It contains no saving power, neither does it relieve us from a single temptation, and is the starting point of spiritual growth from infancy to manhood. Washing the body can never cleanse the heart, yet it is a type of the inward cleansing, and I recommend the same for spiritual children who are unable to bear the strong meat of the Word as I do the hobbyhorse for literal ones. I fear a large majority of those who profess to be Christians to-day never get beyond the baptismal waters, and like the child, spend their lives riding on a single yard of carpet, and like the man referred to, are heirs to vast estates but have not enough spiritual ability to enable them to possess them or realize their privileges. Paul was ever urging his converts to grow, and said in Hebrews 6: "Therefore leaving the principles of the doctrines of Christ let us go on unto perfection; not laying again the foundation of repentance from dead work and faith toward God of the doctrine of baptism and of laying on of hands and of resurrection of the dead and of eternal judgment." Just before this, he says: "We have many things to say and hard to be uttered, seeing ye are dull of hearing, for when ye ought to be teachers ye have need that one teach you again the first principles of the oracles of God, and are become such as have need of milk and not of strong meat, for every one that uses milk is unskillful in the word of righteousness, for he is a babe."

These words of Paul apply to the church of to-day with as much force as it did to the Hebrew Christians in his day, and to pulpit as well as the pew, and to the D. D. and LL. D. as well as the Rev.

All children's toys have their proper use. A hobby horse is safe if used on the nursery carpet, but I would not recommend it as a coaster nor on a toboggan slide. There is also a proper way to use the shadow of baptism, and its typical meaning is washing before eating (of the Lord's supper). The Jews never ate except they first washed. One Lord's day afternoon I attended a pedobaptist meeting, after which the minister addressed me on the subject of immersion. I told him the Jews went from Jerusalem to Jordan to be baptised of John, because there was much water there, and I had seen four adult persons baptised that forenoon in a pint bowl and there was enough water left to baptise the whole congregation in the same way, and Jerusalem must have been a dry place if they had to go all the way to Jordan to get a pint of water to be baptised in. Do your servants who come in from weeding the garden prepare themselves for dinner by putting the ends of their fingers in a pint of water and touching their foreheads. Tertullian, who is the holiest and wisest of the Apostolic Fathers, has written amply on baptism during the second century. He says: " When we are going to enter the water, but a little before, in the presence of the congregation and under the hand of the president, we solemnly profess that we disown the devil, his pomp and his angels, whereupon we are thrice immersed, making a somewhat ampler pledge than the Lord had appointed in the gospel. Then we are taken up as new-born babes; we taste first of all a mixture of milk and honey (the only sweet of those times), and from that day we refrain from the daily bath for a whole week. We take also before daylight, from the hands of the president, the sacrament of the Eucharist." Hypolitus, another of the early

Fathers, confirms this, and says the three immersions are in honor of the Trinity, in whose name they are immersed. Tertullian gives one chapter on presumptious baptism after faithless repentance. He says: "Who will grant to you, a man of so faithless repentance, one single sprinkling of any water whatever? To approach it by stealth, indeed; to get a minister appointed over this business misled by you is easy, but God takes foresight of his own treasure and suffers not the unworthy to steal a march upon it. What, in fact, does he say? Nothing hid that shall not be revealed. Draw whatever veil of darkness you please over your deeds, God is light." This is the only reference he makes to sprinkling, but it explains the position of the church at his day on the subject.

Tertullian died at an advanced age, A. D. 220, and with him, it might be said, died the Apostolic spirit and power of the church. The next important writer was Cyprian, who became Bishop of Carthage, A. D. 248, and was beheaded 258. He is credited with planting many errors in the church which have since remained with it, and the 82 epistles he has left gives a very clear view of his teachings. He was the first to change the Apostolic form of baptism, which was first done by sanctioning clinic baptism for the sick. A young man was converted on what was believed his deathbed. Not being able to be taken to the fount he was baptised by pouring a large quantity of water over him. When he recovered the question arose whether the baptism was sufficient or if he should not be rebaptised by immersion, and the dispute was settled by Cyprion, who decided clinic baptism was sufficient and for the first time established it in the church. He raised baptism to a saving ordinance by removing the substance of baptism and putting the shadow in its place. He next decided that a quantity of water was not necessary and sprinkling was as good as pouring, for which he became a strong advocate. The Episcopal Bishop of Buffalo, A. C. Cox, American editor of "The Fathers," says: "St. Cyprion seems to be the earliest apologist for sprinkling." When he raised skin washing to a saving ordinance, without which none could be saved, he made it necessary that all should be washed, and established for the first, infant baptism, of which Tertullian makes no mention. If he did he would have to explain how an infant could renounce the devil and his pomp although they might be able to take the milk and honey all right.

To baptise a person before he is converted would be like washing an infant before it is born, for we are not born into spiritual life or become a babe in Christ before our conversion. Palestine is repeatedly called the land flowing with milk and honey which is only true in a spiritual sense, and was the only place that the Lord permitted the Jews to fully establish the law of Moses, but never became the permanent home of the Christians. As the milk and honey is infants' food, so the law could only produce spiritual infants, who stood precisely where the convert does to-day, only it is our privilege to go on to perfection while they were obliged to remain infants and live on infants' food, for the blood of bulls and goats could not make the comers thereof perfect, while we are looking for a better country and better fare than milk and honey, for he says: "In this mountain shall the Lord of hosts make unto all people a feast of fat things, a feast of wines on the lees, of fat things full of marrow, of wines on the lees well refined," and Christ said: "I will compel you to sit down and gird myself and serve you." But not with milk and honey.

I have come to those things that are hard to be uttered, seeing you are dull of hearing, but by your ability to hear I can judge of your spiritual growth. Christ said: "He who will come after me let him take up his cross and follow me;" also, "I have another baptism to be baptised with, and how am I strengthened until it is accomplished." This was a baptism of blood, for we are called by water and chosen by blood. Paul says: "Ye have not yet resisted unto blood striving against sin, and ye have forgotten the exhortation which speaketh unto you as unto children. My son despise not the chastening of the Lord, nor faint when thou are rebuked of him, for whom the Lord loveth he chasteneth, and scourgeth every son whom he receiveth. But if ye be without chastisement whereof all sons are partakers, then are ye bastards and not sons, for you must be a son to inherit a crown. Also he says: "The Spirit himself beareth witness with our spirit that we are the children of God; and if children then heirs of God and joint heirs with Christ. (Mark on what condition.) If so be that we suffer with him that we may also be glorified together. For I reckon that the suffering of this present time is not worthy to be compared to the glory that shall be revealed in us." So you see by receiving this blood baptism we not only become sons and heirs but perfect, for Peter says: "He who has suffered in the flesh has ceased from sin. Tertullian's chapter on the subject entitled of the second baptism of blood. We have a second font of blood of which the Lord said, "I have to be baptised with." A baptism when he had been baptised already, for He had come by means of water and blood, just as John has written that he baptised by the water, glorified by the blood, to make us in like manner called by water and chosen by blood. These two baptisms He sent out from the wounds in His pierced side in order that they who believed in His blood might be bathed in the water; they who have been bathed in the water might likewise drink the blood. This is the baptism that doth stand in lieu of the fontal bathing when that has not been received, and restores it when lost.

Another holy Father has written a grand article on the three baptisms. It is too long to give you here, but will copy a sentence: "Assuredly both in water and none the less in their own blood, and then especially in the Holy Spirit, men may be baptised." So you see we are called by water and chosen by blood, but we read, many are called but few chosen. Are you too dull of hearing to take this in? If you are not and wish to, get the Spirit and he will make it plain. But if you think where ignorance is bliss it is folly to be wise, then bring out your hobbyhorse and jolt yourself on that yard of nursery carpet until you are called to the feast of milk and honey, while we feast on the fat things full of marrow.

We read that an angel visited the waters of Bethesda and healed them, and who was immersed in them was healed. Now if some of the water sprinkled on a person healed him why did the helpless man lie so long waiting for some one to put him in if a few drops sprinkled in his face would have healed him? He certainly could have got that. Tertullian gives instances of angels visiting baptismal waters, and adds: "Why have we abducted these instances lest any think too hard for belief that a holy angel of God should grant his presence to water to temper them to man's salvation, while the evil angel holds frequent profane commerce with the selfsame element to man's ruin, as at Galveston.

On the morning of the day I was baptised in New York Bay, one filled with the Spirit and gifted with heavenly visions saw a number of angels hovering over the baptismal waters. I know the humanly taught theologian does not believe in angel's visits, but if they would live the twelfth chapter of Hebrews to the 22nd verse they would say with Paul: "We have come to an innumerable company of angels." And angel's visits are not as few and far between as they imagine. Christ gave the Jews the credit of cleansing the outside, while the Pedobaptists cleanse neither the out or inside. Water cleans the outside and blood the inside. This washing, Paul says, is not joyous, but grievous, but it brings the peaceful fruits of righteousness to those that exercised thereby, for our light affliction, which is but for a moment, worketh for us a far more exceeding and eternal weight of glory. But these are not milksops nor babies' playthings. After we have thoroughly washed ourselves we are ready for the feasting, although I know of a church that feasts them and washes them after.

ELEVENTH STEP.

Communion.

Which also is a trinket for babes to play with, to be received directly after water baptism. It is clear to thinking people that a bite of bread and a sip of wine cannot take away sin any more than the blood of bulls and goats can, which were types of the carnal nature of the sinner. Our theologians eroneously refer them to Christ, but he was nowhere called a bull or a goat, but a lamb, which is also the type of the true follower of Christ, who said to Peter: "If thou lovest me feed my lambs;" and says he will separate the righteous from the wicked, putting the sheep on the right hand, and says to them, "Come, ye blessed of my father," and the goats on the left, saying, "Depart, ye cursed." Also he says, "I will visit the flock and punish the goats." A kid was given as the price of adultery, as in Gen. 38: 17-20, and Judges 15:1. The scapegoate typifies under the law those who escape the baptism of blood. Those who are made perfect by suffering are typified by the goat that was slain, which typify the destruction of our carnal nature which we received from Adam's fall.

When the church had made baptism a saving ordinance they transferred the corruptible elements of the Lord's supper to the literal body and blood of Christ, forgetting that Christ had but one literal body and they could not eat him up without turning cannibals, forgetting that his body is not large enough to go around so that each who pretended to eat of his body at each communion could have a taste. Pious sinners slew him and ever since they have turned cannibals and have been eating him, and they did the first with as much sanctity as they do the last. Christ did not say in reference to the supper, this is my literal body, but this is my body and blood of the New Testament. Testament means law. That is, Christ's death and resurrection established a new way of salvation by which only we can obtain his kingdom which was closed until he opened it. So in communing we neither eat Christ literally nor spiritually, for we do not receive the Holy Spirit by it, but typically the same as water baptism is a type of the blood, which is the inward cleansing, so communion is a type of the spiritual eating of Christ, which we cannot do until these temples are literally cleansed from all filthiness of the flesh by the baptism of the cleansing blood. Having thus washed we are ready to eat and Christ is as ready to be eaten, for he says: "As many as I love I rebuke and chasten. Be zealous therefore and repent. Behold I stand at the door and knock. If any man hear my voice and open the door I will come in to him and will sup with him and be with him. To him that overcometh will I grant to sit with me in my throne even as I overcome and am sit down with my father in his throne. He that hath an ear let him hear what the spirit saith unto the churches." But I fear I am talking to people without ears, for only those who have received the spirit can hear. When we have received the blood we have left the water baptism behind. When we have filled ourselves with the substance we no longer hunger after the shadow. I have now given you the meaning of the two ordinances out of which so much error, dispute, persecution and bloodshed has come.

Henry the VIII of England was the first to establish Protestantism in England, which grew out of a dispute with the Pope, and was organized on Catholic doctrine, only he denied the supremacy of the Pope and put himself in his place, but consented to have the bible circulated but refused to let people think for themselves, so he passed what is called the bloody six articles. The first was The Real Presence of Christ in the Eucharist and Transubstantiation. That is, the bread become the real body of Christ and the substance of which it was made no longer exists in it. A woman that made wafers for the priest's communion said in presenting them: " You say that after you bless them none of the original substance remains." He answered that all would be changed into the literal body of Christ. She replied: " I put some arsenic poison in them, but if it is changed it will not hurt you." It is needless to add that his faith failed.

All who disputed, wrote or preached against the first article were to suffer the death penalty and forfeit all of their goods to the crown without being allowed to rescind or recant. Under this law, Thos. Cromwell, uncle of Oliver and the greatest reformer of his day, Chief Secretary of England, Master of the Rule and Vice General of English Monasteries, which he suppressed, and did more to circulate the Bible than any other man in his day, lost his head and estate for violating this legal dogma, with many others. Naughty children to play with innocent toys in this cruel way. Martin Luther stuck to this dogma until he came near rendering the church he had formed and admitted on his death bed that he had carried his arguments too far.

While I believe in and recommend these ordinances to the spiritual babes, I find the Lord receives and blesses the Quakers, who reject them, and those who live up to their faith, live and die happy, proving they are not essential to salvation. But we had not better be baptized until we fully believe, for what is not of faith is sin. A man who had preached for the M. E.'s 12 years and sprinkled hundreds was convinced of the error, and was asked at the baptismal waters if he ever saw a candidate show any evidence of receiving a blessing at sprinkling. He replied he did not, but I see unmistakable proofs of it here at this immersion. So the only road to the kingdom is, first, to be converted; second, to be baptized; third, to partake of the Lord's supper; fourth, to receive the Holy Spirit; fifth, who will lead us if we allow him to lead, to the baptism of blood or chastening of the Lord; sixth, which will open the door for Christ to enter our hearts when we will in a spiritual sense eat his flesh and drink his blood, for he will dwell within us., and we can say with Paul, I am crucified with Christ; nevertheless, I live; yet not I, but Christ liveth in me; and the life which I now live in the flesh; I live by the faith of the Son of God, who loved me, and gave himself for me. While these ordinances are sacred and should be taken with solemnity, they should not be received for more than they are worth. A few years ago some young men met to hold a communion in mockery. God visited them and one or more were smitten with death.

If you have followed me thus far and say (as some have) that you do not want Christ's kingdom if you have to give up the pleasures and vanities of this life to obtain it, and prefer to run the risk of the great tribulation and eternal judgment, or think you are strong enough to scale the battlements of Heaven and take it by force, you are deceiving yourself, and we had better part company here, for it is useless for you to follow me farther, for I fail to see how I can serve you farther, only to pray that the Holy Spirit will convict you and show you where you stand. But on the other hand if you have counted the cost and are willing to pay it, but fear you will not be able to enter in if you try, I tell you your fears are groundless, for Christ said, "He that asketh receiveth and he that seeketh findeth and to him that knocketh the door is open." This applies to the most hardened sinner as well as the most popular preacher or the most noted church official. If you have not started commence at the first of the seven steps given above. If this book has not made your way clear send for my other (see preface). If you have not started, start now, for the time is limited and you cannot go over the road in one day. The battle at most will be a short one and the victory most glorious. To ministers I say, if you accept the truth you will have to preach it, and it may cost you your pulpit; but if you are faithful you will take the worthiest of your members with you, and your bread is sure. So you have nothing to fear but all to gain.

TWELFTH STEP.

The Sabbath vs. The Lord's Day.

The Sabbath was made for man. After I had resolved to follow the Lord at any cost I kept the Jews' Sabbath for a year, because I failed to find any authority in our Bible for observing the Lord's day, and I read the Seventh Day Adventist publications on the subject. But when I learned that some of the most important books of the New Testament had been suppressed, as well as the works of the early Fathers by the corrupt church, I was led to look more carefully into the subject and found important errors in the teachings of the Adventists. The most important is that the early church kept the seventh day until Constantine passed a law compelling them to observe the Lord's day, which was about A. D. 325. I am prepared to prove that the Lord's day and not the Sabbath was observed from the days of the Apostles and even by the Apostles themselves. But we will first consider the meaning and God's purpose in instituting it.

We read that God made the world in six days and rested on the Sabbath, which means seventh, for Theophilus, who lived in the early part of the second century, says, "Concerning the seventh day, which all men acknowledge but the most know not what among the Hebrews is called the Sabbath, is translated into Greek the seventh; a name that is adopted by every nation although they know not the reason of the application." So those who call the first day of the week the Sabbath are in error. The Catholic church claims the honor of changing the Sabbath from the seventh to the first day, but they have no foundation for such a claim nor authority for such a change, for a church cannot date back of its creed, which was first made at the Nicene Council, A. D. 325, in which council they threw both Peter and his faith overboard but still claim to build on him. One who followed Christ and one of the seventy that he sent out to preach, and is called the spiritual father of Paul, and was for many years his companion in his labor, of whom Christ said: "Separate me Barnabas and Paul for the work whereunto I have called them." Putting Barnabas first, giving him the preference. We are apt to speak of them as Paul and Barnabas, but in Acts their names occur 12 times, and 9 times Barnabas' name is mentioned first, giving him the preference. His epistle was canonized by the church for 300 years and attributed to him and quoted from as scripture. In the Sinai codex, which is supposed to be the oldest Bible, it is with the other books of the New Testament, but later it was suppressed because of some strong truths that it taught, and an effort was made to prove that it was written later by another man by that name. I quote from the introduction: "Origin describes it as a Catholic epistle," and seems to rank it among the Catholic epistles. Other statements have been quoted from the Fathers to show that they held this to be an authentic production of the Apostle Barnabas, and certainly no other name is hinted at in Christian antiquity as that of the writer. His worst enemies admit that he is an authentic writer of the early church, and cannot date him later than the early part of the second century, for he was quoted as early as that and that is sufficient to prove the position of the Antenicene church on the Sabbath question. The 15th chapter is devoted to that subject, a part of which I will quote. "The Sabbath is mentioned at the beginning of the creation, thus: And God made in six days the works of his hands and made an end on the seventh day, and rested on it and sanctified it. Attend, my children, to the meaning of this expression: He finished in six days. This implies that the Lord will finish all things in six thousand years, for a day is with him a thousand years. And he himself testifies, saying, behold to-day will be a thousand years, therefore in six days, that is, in six thousand years, all things will be finished. And he rested on the seventh day. This meaneth when his son cometh again he shall destroy the time of the wicked man and judge the ungodly and change the sun, moon and stars, then shall He truly rest on the seventh day. Moreover He says, "Thou shall sanctify it with pure hands and a pure heart." If therefore any one can now sanctify the day which God has sanctified unless he is pure in heart in all things, we are deceived. One properly resting sanctifies it, when we ourselves having received the promise, wickedness no longer existing, and all things having been made new by the Lord, shall he be able to work righteousness. Then we shall begin to sanctify it, having been first sanctified ourselves. Further he says to them: "Your new moons and your Sabbaths I cannot endure." You perceive how he speaks. Your present Sabbaths are not acceptable to me, but that is what I have made, namely this, when giving rest to all things I shall make the beginning of the eighth day—that is the beginning of another world. Wherefore, also, we keep the eighth day with joyfulness, the day also on which Jesus rose from the dead."

Some try to prove that He told them to put the Sabbath away because they did not keep the rest of the law. Let them prove if they can if God ever forbade them to keep any part of the law before he put it away. They obey in dropping the feast of the new moon, why not the Sabbath as well. They say that the Sabbath was included in the ten commandments and they were never to be annulled. But that is not so, for the second read: "I will visit the iniquities of the fathers upon the children unto the third and fourth generation." That was given to bar the kingdom until Christ came to open it, for if perfection had been under the law Christ's coming would have been unnecessary, but if a man was perfect like Joshua, the sin of his father or grandfather could have been brought against him, and when Christ came it was no longer necessary, for he opened the door, so we read in Jeremiah 31: "In those days shall they say no more. The fathers have eaten a sour grape and the children's teeth are set on edge. But every one shall die for his own iniquity; every man that eateth the sour grape his teeth shall be set on edge."

The six days typify the 6,000 years, and the sevent, Christ's reign with his saints, which is our privilege to share, while those who keep the Sabbath will be our subjects for, and we observe the eighth or first in honor of the time when Christ shall restore the kingdom to Him and He commence his eternal reign. To observe the seventh day would be self worship, or bowing to the throne on which we sit, for Christ says: "He who overcomes shall sit on my throne." So the Sabbath was not changed but annulled, and the Lord's day instituted for a different purpose and on a different principle. There is no command to abstain from work which Christ tried to teach the Jews, and he was blamed more for refusing to observe it after their law than anything else. Christ taught us to do well, not nothing on the Sabbath day. I will quote from some of the rest of the Fathers to show how they observe it for the benefit of those who are not willing to receive the epistle of Barnabas:

"This custom of not bending the knee on Sunday is a symbol of the resurrection through which we have been set free by the grace of Christ from sin and from death, which has been put to death under him. Now this custom took its rise from the Apostolic times, as the blessed Prenaeus, the martyr and Bishop of Lyons, declare He was a disciple and companion of the Apostle John."

Peter, Bishop of Alexandria, says: "But on the Lord's day we ought not to fast, for it is the day of joy for the resurrection of the Lord, and on it, says he, we ought not to even bow the knee."

Bordessa says: "On one day, the first of the week, we assemble ourselves together."

Tertullian, A. D. 150: "The Holy Spirit upbraided the Jews with their holy days. Your Sabbaths and new moons, saith he, my soul hateth. We to whom Sabbaths are strange and the new moons formerly beloved of God. Of the Jews he says: O bitter fidelity to the notions of their own sects which claim no solemnity of the Christians for itself for the Lord's day nor Pentecost, even if they had known them would they have shared them with us; for they would fear lest they would seem to be Christians. We are not apprehensive lest we seem to be heathens."

So we see the Sabbath was not changed, but annulled, and the Lord's day instituted for an entirely different purpose to commemorate the risen Lord and the commencement of God's eternal reign. As the Jews were taught to observe the Sabbath to commemorate Christ and his brethren's reign over them during the seventh millenium, so we are to observe the eighth day in honor to the eighth millenium, when we will resign our crowns for something better; for of the increase of His government there will be no end.

Since the time of the Nicene council the church rejected Christ's cross for themselves, which caused them to go back to the spirit of the law if not the letter, and consequently they lose the crown and Christ will avail them nothing. For them the Sabbath is proper, but if we desire to reign with Christ we must pass over millennial worship and honor God's reign beyond. I have observed that spiritual people who go back to Sabbath observance lose their spiritual power. One of the leaders of the Seventh Day Church left it a few years ago and gave for a reason that the blessing did not follow its observance. Attempts to legislate men into the Kingdom of Heaven have proved a failure, for we cannot compel men to be holy. Law makers who try to compel men who think it is their duty to rest on the seventh day in obedience to the fourth commandment, make them break it by resting on the first, for it says, six days shalt thou labor, and we cannot labor six days of the week and rest two, and God's "shalt" is just as imperative as his "shalt not." And we are commanded to work as well as rest; and all such laws are unconstitutional, for our state and national constitution gives us religious liberty.

The day commences at sunset, for the evening and the morning was the first day, and the day typifies the history of the ages. The beautiful sunset was the newly created world, but sin brought darkness of the antediluvian world. Moses with the law brought the dawn, and Christ the noonday, and the millennium the sunset, but there will be no night to follow, for it does not say the evening and morning makes the seventh day, for it will close with the beginning of God's glorious reign.

The Fathers unanimously taught the observance of the Lord's day, not particularly as a day of rest, but of joy. One says, he who fasts on that day is guilty of the blood and body of Christ. A day of alms giving. Upon the first day of the week let every one lay by him in store as God hath prospered him, that there be no gathering when I come—1 Cor. 16:2. It was also the day on which they held their meetings.

Tertullian, A. D. 150, says: "It follows, accordingly, that in so far as abolition of carnal circumcision and of the old law is demonstrated as having been consummated at its specific time, so also the observance of the Sabbath is demonstrated to have been temporary. And through this arises the question for us, what Sabbath God wills us to keep. For the Scripture points to a Sabbath eternal and a Sabbath temporal. For Isaiah says, your Sabbath my soul hateth, and in another place, my Sabbath ye have profaned. Whence we discern that the temporal Sabbath is human, and the eternal Sabbath is accounted divine."

THIRTEENTH STEP.

Eating and Drinking.

Whither therefore ye eat, or drink, or whatever ye do, do all to the glory of God.—1 Cor. 10: 31.

I address those who eat to live, not those who live to eat. I find many who profess the worthy name of Christ who are unwilling to make any sacrifice of their appetite for His sake and never forego a tempting meal for the sake of fasting, even when their impaired health requires it. God never withheld anything from his people that was for their good, and abstaining from food from 18 to 24 hours once or twice a week is promotive of health. A disarrangement of the stomach and bowels is generally corrected by such a fast. I know of a number who use no other remedy, and sometimes prolong it from 24 to 48 hours if necessary. I recently read of a minister who fasted for 40 days from the advice of his physician, to cure prolonged stomach trouble, with good results. To keep those organs healthy it is necessary to give them frequent rest. Perhaps no class needs more warning on this subject than ministers, for when they call upon us we are apt to set the richest but not the most wholesome food before them, and their service does not require enough bodily exercise to aid its digestion, so many are afflicted with dyspepsia and gout, from which Spurgeon died. Inquiring for Moody in a crowd, I was told he was the big man. Most ministers show the result of high living.

If we desire to approach near unto God we must

abstain from all of the appetites of the body to drive out the unembodied evil spirits that inhabit our bodies, as Paul teaches in 1 Cor. 7: 5. But this was only milk for babes. As an example for us Christ continued his fast 40 days during His temptation to starve the demons out. No wonder they wanted the stones turned to bread, but when they failed they left Him.

Clemment of Alexandria, an able writer of the second century, wrote a valuable article on this subject. He says: "Some men live that they may eat, as the irrational beings whose life is their bellies and nothing else, but the instructor enjoins us to eat that we may live." People dare to call by the name of food their dabbling in luxuries, which glide into mischieveous pleasure. Antophanus, the Delian physician, said that this variety of viands was the one cause of disease. For my part I am sorry for this disease; while they are not ashamed to sing the praises of their delicacies. Altering these by means of condiments the gluttons gape for the sauces. Whatever the earth and the depth of the sea and the unmeasured space of the air produce, they cater for their gluttony. In their greed and solicitude, the gluttons seem to sweep the world with a drag-net to gratify their luxurious tastes. These gluttons surrounded with the sound of the hissing frying-pan and wearing their whole life away at the pestle and mortar cling to matter like fire. More than that, they emasculate plain food, namely bread, by straining off the nutritious part of the grain so that the necessary part of food becomes matter of luxury. There is no limit to epicurism among men. For it has driven them to sweetmeats, honey cakes and sugar plums, inventing a multitude of desserts, hunting after all manner of dishes. A man like this seems to me to be all jaw and nothing else. Desire not, says the scripture, rich men's dainties, for they belong to a false and base life, they partake of luxurious dishes which a little after go to the dunghill. But we who seek the heavenly bread must rule the belly, which is beneath heaven, and much more the things which are agreeable to it, which God shall destroy, says the apostle, justly execrating gluttonous desires. For it is not seemly that we, after the passions of the rich man's son in the gospel, should as prodigally abuse the father's gift; but we should use them without undue attachment to them, as having command over ourselves. For we are enjoined to rule over meats, not to be slaves to them. Any food or drink that has a tendency to bring us under its power is unhealthy and should not be used. I refer to such as tea, coffee, fermented and distilled liquors, snuff and tobacco.

Many contend that the law given in Leviticus, 11th chapter, does not apply to the Christian age and modern church, but the truth is the modern church is neither Jewish nor Christian, they neither obey the law nor the gospel. They go back to the law to justify themselves in going to war, living in sin, taking usury and many other things which the gospel precludes; but reject it in eating meats forbidden in the law but not referred to in the gospel, because the Jews were more strenuous observers of the law of eating then as they are now and need no teaching in Christ's time on that subject. But the church now lusts after forbidden meats and excuses itself by saying we are not Jews, while it would be hard for them to explain what they are.

Nothing is more strenuously forbidden than swine's flesh, yet nothing is used by the church with greater impunity. No part of the law was annulled except the parts that were expressed in the writings of the prophets or apostles. Isaiah was more a prophet of the new law than the old, and we have not to refer to the New Testament for authority to put away the Sabbath, sacrifices, incense and feasts, once dear to the Jews but abandoned by us, for Isaiah has told us. But what authority has he given us to eat swine's flesh and other forbidden meats? The two last chapters refer to not only the gospel age but the last days of it and the millennium, as any one can plainly see. He says: "A people that provoke me to anger continually. That eat swine's flesh, and broth of abominable things is in their vessels. Which say, stand by thyself for I am holier than thou. these are a smoke in my nose, a fire that burneth all the day. For behold the Lord will come with fire. and with his chariots like a whirlwind, to render his anger with fury. and his rebuke with flames of fire. For by fire and by his sword will the Lord plead with all flesh. and the slain of the Lord shall be many. They that sanctify themselves and purify themselves in the garden behind one tree in the midst, eating swine's flesh and the abomination, and the mouse shall be consumed together saith the Lord. For I know their thoughts; it shall come that I will gather all nations and tongues; and they shall come and see my glory." As these prophecies are not yet fulfilled the punishment of the swine eaters are as yet future.

God did not make this law because he wanted to be arbitrary and hold from man things that were good for him. but because they were not. All physicians forbid their patients to eat swine's flesh. One of the best learned in the country told me that the law of eating was one of the proofs of the inspiration of the bible. for its sanitary teaching was far in advance of medical science of that age. and if people observed it more they would enjoy better health and live much longer. It is said that the average life of a Jew is nearly a third longer than that of a Christian. and no other reason can be given than his following the diet ordained of God. A public clambake was given here, and I heard that most of the partakers were sick next day. Christ sent the devils in a herd of 2,000 swine, and caused their destruction, and the Gadarenes like many of to-day, ordered him out of their country. Dr. Foot says the best use to employ swine to is to drown devils. If swine is good for food, then Christ committed a great sin in destroying so much wholesome food, and He who gathered up the fragments that nothing be lost had at once become extravagantly wasteful, but if the Gadarenes were wrongly keeping forbidden and injurious property, Christ was justifiable in destroying it.

Ex-Governor Flower accumulated many millions by his wise investments, but when he invested in pork he did not make the fortune that Colonel Sellers dreamed of, for he found he had taken on a load that he could not unload, for his freight handlers went on a strike and all of his trusts could do nothing for him, and there was nothing left for him to do but to "pass in his checks and go to probate." But for that unwise investment he might have still been adding to his millions. The facts are he came in from fishing, said he was hungry as a horse, called for ham and radishes, ate heartily, and was taken sick before he left the table and died from indigestion in a few hours. Soon after an article appeared in a New York newspaper against swine eating, and a man calling himself a doctor tried to answer it in Rural New Yorker, but admitted enough against swine eating to upset his theory. He said it took longer to digest pork than other meats (4 hours). That the Jews lived longer than the swine eaters (a third), and gave as a reason that they adhered to Moses' bill of fare and they did not work as hard. I suppose he meant their digestive organs. He said he had more calls to see people made sick by eating veal than pork. That may be. Veal is easily digested and physics some, and is good for those who are troubled with costiveness; and some cannot take physic without calling a physician; but it leaves no lasting effect as pork does. If it does not agree with you do not eat it. I know a man who cannot eat strawberries without being poisoned, but that is no reason why I should not eat them.

If you burn a candle at both ends it will soon be extinguished. Will we be if we do two things at once? We cannot speak, think, or move without wasting the part of the body exercised, and the blood, which is the body constructor, rushes there to repair the loss, or at least to support it, and if it repaired it fully we would never tire. A druggist's scale is better to weigh grains on than a coal dealer's, and a weak man is a better judge of what exhausts than a giant. Being the former I am a competent judge. If I walk up hill and talk at the same time I tire in half of the time that I do when I do but one, because I have but one blood and that has to be divided. An athlete that wins a race will not speak while running. During digestion a supply of blood is necessary to support the digestive organs, so we cannot work best during that period. During sleep the heart beats slower than when we labor, which gives that rest. We should eat a light, easily digested supper at least an hour before retiring, then during sleep the blood will restore the part that wasted by the day's work. I have spent an evening studying a lesson and retired without being able to repeat a line, but in the morning before I arose I could repeat a whole page, because digestion had ceased and all losses had been replaced and my memory was perfect. As it takes 4 hours to digest pork and we eat it 3 times a day, as many do, we lay out 12 hours' work for our digestive organs, which will soon wear them out. We would complain bitterly if our masters kept us at work 7 days in the week. It would be better for us to eat easily-digested food and not go to work until after digestion, which would be nearly accomplished during the hour's nooning. If swine eaters did that they would not have enough time left to earn their hog.

Did God forbid its eating to deprive us of a blessing, or for our good? If the latter, you cannot blame him for consuming the suicides who eat it at the sacrifice of one-third of their lives. I know several who have received the spirit who have been forbidden to eat it by him. This applies equally to other forbidden meats.

FOURTEENTH STEP.

Ye are God's.

Jesus answered them: "Is it not written in your law, I say, ye are God's?"
If he called them God's unto whom the word of God came, and the scripture cannot be broken.—John 10: 14-35.

If a man called himself a God he would be treated as an imposter or a lunatic, yet the scripture cannot be broken. When we look upon frail man and the stupendous works of art we are inspired to say, "What hath God wrought?" The inventive genius of a nation can be measured by its faith in God. Some of our most useful discoveries is the result of a dream. A shotmaker dreamed that it rained shot; then he thought a drop of water formed a globe and hail was round; so he took some melted lead to the top of the church tower and poured it in a tub of water below and took out the finest shot he ever saw. Placing the eye of the sewing machine needle at the point was the result of a dream.

When Edison made his first phonograph, he was so much surprised at the result that he doubted his ability to build a second. Yet these men were not gods, for their inventions were in the scope of human power; but I assert with all boldness that it is in every man's power to be a god; yet you might have to rake the whole world with a drag-net to catch one. A god is known, not by his words but by his works. When John the Baptist sent to know if he was the Christ, he proved his godhead by the miracles he was performing. God said to Moses: "See, I have made thee a god to Pharaoh." His divinity he proved by bringing all the plagues on the Egyptians; turning daylight into pitchy darkness, dividing the sea, drawing water out of the flinty rock, and many others that the united power of the world could not accomplish. An inventor in a fit of ecstasy, proclaimed, "Show me where I can place my prop and I will shake the world." He who will place it on the rock Christ Jesus will not only shake the earth but heaven also.

Commodianus in speaking of Antechrist and the two last prophets, says: "The whole earth on every side shall tremble for seven years. The earth turns on its axis from west to east at the rate of about 25,000 miles a day. Joshua caused it to stop and stand still for about a day. Isaiah did more. He not only stopped its motion but reversed it. Elijah called down fire from heaven, divided the Jordan, and did many other things that only a God could do. Elisha was not least among the gods. He could smite an army with blindness and restore their sight, call down fire and consume his enemies, and not only raise the dead, but there was vitality enough in his bones after death to bring a dead man to life as soon as he touched them. The three Holy Children were able to quench the violence of fire. Pollycarp, John's disciple was uninjured in a furious fire when they tried to burn him, and John himself refused to cook when they threw him into a caldron of boiling oil. These miracles none but a god could perform. The Apostles could both heal the sick with the word and raise the dead. I told you that Christ proved His divinity by His works and said: "He that believeth on me the works that I do shall he do also, and greater works than these shall he do because I go to my father."

I said it is any man's privilege to be a god. God

says: "Behold, I make all things new." Suppose the world and contents were destroyed and you alone was left to recreate, let us see what kind of world you would make. Of course we will assume that you know more than the Creator and would produce a better one. You would level the mountains and hills, pulverize the rocks, turn the vast waste of water into fertile farms and make fishes grow on trees, and make it such a vast plain that a railroad could be built around it without use of pick or shovel. Put the precious metals and stones on the surface and make gold as abundant as stones so it would lose its value and we would have no medium of exchange. It would lose its beauty, as an unbroken plain would be painful to the eye. The landscape painter would come to grief, for when he drew one picture he would have it all; and where would the boys go to coast? When you went to create electricity you would find you do not know as much as the Creator, for it would bother you to make what you do not know what it is or tell what it is made of. When you reproduced vegetation you of course would leave out thorns and thistles and noxious weeds, we would have a rose without a thorn. But these were the result of Adam's sin and have been good to keep men out of mischief, for there is some mischief still for idle hands to do. You would bring back the domestic animals, as you would need the horse, cow, sheep, dog and fowls. But the cat would be superfluous, as there would be no rats or mice for them to catch, and the maneaters would be left behind. But I fail to see how the disobedient prophet or the 42 children who mocked at Elisha were to be punished, if it had not been for the lion and the bear. To go into details and relate all the improvements ye gods would make would make my discourse tedious, but it will be the new earth, too grand to be conceived of or be compared with this. We will go a step higher. You will want servants to do your bidding and run errands, of sufficient intelligence to converse and perform faithful service. To fill this place the Lord created the angels, and it would bother you to improve on them. For two reasons they differed from the animal creation; they weere immortal and were all created of one sex, so they would have no ambition but to serve their Lord.

Then to crown all you would want a friend companion, a companion created after your image and likeness. Not your superior, lest he would reign over you, but a little lower, so you could keep your supremacy. 8th Psalm, 5th verse, R. V. reads of man: "For thou hast made him but a little lower than God and crowned him with glory and honor." I see where you can make a grand improvement on God's plan of creation, who left woman for or after all else was created and the six days' creation was ended. You of course would want a wife, and instead of leaving her for the last you would create her as soon as you had a place to put her, and as you are a god you are not subject to any law as you are a law unto yourself and cannot do an unholy thing. And as your nature calls for more than one wife you would make for yourself not less than King Solomon had, as you have a pride not to be outdone in these things. And as for your counsellors and companions you would follow the plan of the eastern kings, who multiply wives and make all men eunuchs to prevent jealousy as well as their getting your wives away from you. If you did not you would not be following your own natural propensities. You might make a mighty god to the heathens, for their gods had many wives and begot many children. In mythology we read Jupiter had many wives, among which was Juno, his own sister, and had many children and was father of men and the gods, but some of their goddesses were virgins, among which was Dianna, to whose honor the great temple of the Ephesus was built; also Minerva and Iris. To these they bestowed the greatest honor. But I fear you would not be accounted worthy to reign with Christ. Mahommed promised his faithful followers 30 virgins for wives in the next world, but restricted them to the paltry number of four in this, while he took eight for himself.

We will now look into the lives of the nine gods of the Old Testament and see if we can discover the secret of their power. Daniel, who was so tough that the lions could not digest him and was the most beloved by God, who said three times, "Thou are much beloved, Daniel," was an eunuch, as well as his three asbestos companions, Elijah, Elisha, Isaiah. Moses took a wife in his old age, for at 80 he had Jethro's daughter and two small children; so small that they could ride with their mother on an ass. When he went to deliver Israel from Egypt he attempted to take his wife along, which was contrary to God's will, so the Lord met him and tried to slay him. So he was obliged to send her back to her father's hous. It was after that that God said: "I have made thee a god to Pharaoh;" and I guess we will have to leave our wives behind before we can be a god to anyone.

The time had not come to teach virginity, for Christ had reserved that for himself, so the earlier scriptures are not very explicit on the subject. After Moses had led Israel to Sinai, Jethro came and brought his family, which did not resound to the glory of Moses. He was not permitted to take her when he was with the Lord in Sinai 40 days, and he was not permitted to lead Israel over Jordan, nor were his relatives and followers permitted to look on or bury him when he died. But Joshua, a holy virgin and type of Christ, was to take from him his power and honor who was worthy to be numbered among the gods. The prophet Jeremiah married when he was but 13 years old, and had but one daughter, named Hamutal, who married Josiah, who was Judah's last righteous king, who began to reign when 8 years old, and his virtues may be attributed to Jeremiah's influence over him. Jeremiah's wife died when he was still young and the Lord told him not to take another. Ezekiel also was a widower. If Jonah had a wife he did not take her on his missionary journey, as most modern preachers do. I think his celebrity was the secret of his power. Hosea was told to take a wife of whoredom that he might be a sign to Israel who went whoring after ofter gods. There is no evidence that the other minor prophets were married, but they performed no miracles.

When Christ taught virginity, both by example and precept, the Apostolic Fathers tell us that of the disciples Peter was the only one who ever married, and appeared to be a widower in Christ's time, as his mother-in-law kept his house; and he was the first of the twelve to embrace virginity in its fullness, by which he earned the keys to Christ's kingdom. Paul had a wife, which caused the great struggle of Romans, seventh chapter, and 1 Cor. 9: 26. He finally gained the victory as he tells us, by suffering, in Col. 1: 24-29. Now I boldly affirm that it cannot be proved that ever a husband or wife living after the flesh ever proved themselves a god by performing a miracle, even by healing the sick by the laying on the hands in God's name.

The thought of a god having a carnal wife is too ridiculous for any thinking person to accept, unless he is a heathen, whose gods agree with passions of fallen man. Go to all that have had the power to heal the sick in Christ's name during the last 20 years and see if the spirit has not lead to virginity.

I do not mean the so called Christian science, for if they have any power they obtain it of the evil one. If we ever become gods we will have to regain God's nature, which was lost in Adam's fall. 8th Psalm, 5th verse, R. V. says, "Thou has made him but little lower than god and crowned him with glory and honor." II Peter, 1:4, says, "He hath granted unto us his precious and exceeding great promises, that through these ye may become partakers of the divine nature (By marrying? No!), having excaped from the corruption (death) that is in the world by lust." The gods are immortal, "for," says Paul, "if ye live after the flesh ye must die; but if by the spirit ye make to die (marrying) the doings of the flesh, ye shall live." I will now quote the 82nd Psalm to show what will become of your carnal gods if you refuse to accept these truths: "I said, ye are gods and all of you sons of the Most High. Nevertheless ye shall die like men and fall like one of the princes."

FIFTEENTH STEP.

Is the End of the Age and the Coming of the Lord Near?

"The great day of the Lord is near, it is near, it hasteth greatly."—Zeph. 1: 14.

When Christ was asked when his coming and the end would come, he did not answer direct, but told them to get ready to meet him but not to get ready to die. For when we are ready to meet Christ the subject of death will not trouble us, and nothing will stimulate us more to prepare than to tell us the coming of the Lord is at hand. Those who set a date nearer than seven years ahead, as Miller and many others have, show great ignorance of scripture, which plainly teaches that the two witnesses will come seven years before the end to seal the 144,000 virgins, who will be translated three and a half years later, when Antichrist will begin his rule of the world, which will complete seven years, when the world will be burned, as told in this first chapter of Zephaniah. Those teachers who were contemporaries with Christ and the Apostles taught that the end would come just 6,000 years from creation. I will quote what Gibbon in his "Decline and Fall of the Roman Empire" says of the teachings of the early Fathers: "The ancient and popular doctrine of the millennium was intimately connected with the second coming of Christ. As the works of the creation had been finished in six day, their duration in this present state according to the tradition that was attributed to the prophet Elijah, was fixed to six thousand years, and by the same analogy it was inferred that this long period of labor and contention, which was now almost elapsed, would be succeeded by a joyful Sabbath of a thousand years, and that Christ, with the triumphant band of the saints and the elect that had escaped death or who had been miraculously revived, would reign upon earth till the time appointed for the last general resurrection. So pleasing was this hope to the mind of believers that the New Jerusalem, the seat of the blissful kingdom, was quickly adorned with all the gayest colors of the imagination. The assurance of such a millennium was carefully inculcated by a succession of Fathers from Justin Martyr (first century) and Irenatus (second century), who conversed with the immediate disciples of the apostles, down to Lactantius (fourth century), who was preceptor to the son of Constantine. That it might not be universally received it appears to have been the reigning sentiment of the orthodox believers." After the last date he says: " The doctrine of Christ's reign upon earth was at first treated as a profound allegory, was considered by degrees a doubtful and useless opinion, and was at length rejected as the absurd invention of heresy and fanaticism."

Gibbon could find Fathers who lived and wrote on this subject before Justin; Barnabas, a disciple of Christ, who I have quoted elsewhere. Popais, a disciple of John, says: "Clement (Peter's companion) and Pennlenus, the priest of the Alexandrians, and the wise Ammoneus, agreed with each other who understood that the works of six days referred to Christ and the whole church."

Methodius, A. D. 260, says in his Banquet of the Ten Virgins, "God commanded his own son to reveal to the prophets his own future appearance in the world by the flesh, in which the joy and knowledge of the spiritual eighth day should be proclaimed which should bring the remission of sins and the resurrection and that thereby the passions and corruption of men would be circumscribed. For since in six day God made the heavens and the earth and finished the whole world and rested on the seventh day from all his work, that he had made and blessed the seventh day and sanctified it, so by a figure in the seventh month has been gathered in. We are commanded to keep the feast of the Lord, which signifies that when this world shall be terminated on the seven thousand years, when God shall have completed the world, he shall rejoice in us. For I also taking my journey and going forth from the Egypt of this life come first to the resurrection, which is the true feast of tabernacles, and having set up my tabernacle, adorned with the fruits of virtue, on the first day of the resurrection, which is the day of judgment, celebrate with Christ the millennium of rest, which is called the seventh day, even the true Sabbath. Then again, from thence, I, a follower of Jesus, who has entered into the heavens, as they also, after the rest of the feast of tabernacles come into the land of promise, come into the heavens, not continuing to remain in tabernacles; that is, my body not remaining as it was before, but, after the space of a thousand years, changed from the human and corruptible form into angelic size and beauty, whereat last we virgins, when the festival of the resurrection is consummated, shall pass from the wonderful place to the tabernacle of greater and better things, ascending to the very house of God above the heavens."

Hippolytus says: "Since, then, in six days God made all things, it follows that 6000 years must be fulfilled; and they are not yet fulfilled."

Loctantius, A. D. 260, says: "At the commencement of the sacred reign that the prince of the devils will be bound by God. But he also when the thousand years of the kingdom, this is, seven thousand of the world, shall begin to be ended, will be loosed afresh, and being sent forth from prison will go forth and assemble all the nations which shall then be under the dominion of the righteous, that they may make war against the holy city, and there shall be called together from all the world an innumerable company of the nations, and they shall besiege and surround the city. Then the last anger of God shall come upon the nations and utterly destroy them."

I have copied enough from the Fathers to show that the Apostolic church taught unanimously that Christ's second advent and the end of the world would occur at the end of the 6000 years of the world's age, yet I have come far short of exhausting them on the subject, and the next question is, how old is the world? Our reference Bible gives the date of the birth of Christ at 4004 years, and we about 1900 years since, making 5904, which, if correct, would make us wait 96 years; but as the compiler of these dates made no claim of inspiration he might have made a mistake, so we will see if we can discover one.. I Samuel, 10th chapter, tells of the anointing of Saul's kingdom, gives the date 1095 before Christ, which appears correct. He says Joshua divided the land among the tribes 1444 B. C., Judges, 18th chapter. This would make the time of the Judges from the dividing of the land to King Saul 350. If we turn to Acts 13: 19, the inspired apostle says: " He divided the land by lot, and after that he gave them judges about the space of 450 years." Here we see a discrepancy of 100 years, and a close study of the book of Judges will prove the last date nearly right; and if we add the 100 to the 5904 we have 6003. But a slight mistake in some of the dates has been discovered.

I came near forgetting to add what Barbesan wrote on the subject, and was greatly surprised that so good a knowledge of astronomy was obtained so long before the invention of the telescope. I showed it to a professor of astronomy who said it was correct. Barbesan therefore, an aged man and one celebrated for his knowledge of events, wrote concerning the synchronism with another of the luminaries of heaven, speaking as follows:

2 revolutions of Saturn, 60 years.
5 revolutions of Jupiter, 60 years.
40 revolutions of Mars, 60 years.
60 revolutions of the Sun, 60 years.
72 revolutions of Venus, 60 years.
150 revolutions of Mercury, 60 years.
720 revolutions of the Moon, 60 years.

"This," says he, "is one synchronism of them, so that from hence it appears to complete 100 such will require 6000 years, thus:

200 revolutions of Saturn, 6000 years.
500 revolutions of Jupiter, 6000 years.
4000 revolutions of Mars, 6000 years.
6000 revolutions of the Sun, 6000 years.
7200 revolutions of Venus, 6000 years.
15000 revolution of Mercury, 6000 years.
72000 revolutions of the Moon, 6000 years.

These things did Barbesan thus compute when deserting, to show that this work would stand only 6000 years.

SIXTEENTH STEP.

Fools.

"The fool hath said in his heart: No God."—53d Psalm.

"We are fools for Christ's sake, but ye are wise in Christ; we are weak but ye are strong; ye are honorable but are despised—1 Cor. 4: 10.

The world is made up of three different kinds of fools.

First, the big fools. Second, the wise fools. Third, the Lord's fools.

First the big fools, who say in their heart: No God. He does not say it with his mouth, for if you ask him if there is a God he will say without hesitation, yes; but every action belies his words. God has implanted in every man's heart faith in a superior being and a hope and desire for something better beyond the grave. The idolater worships through his wooden god an unseen being, and hopes he will bring him to a heavenly home of immortality beyond the grave. The red man who used to hunt the deer and hare through these vast forests worshiped and did reverence to the Great Spirit of good whose abode is in heaven, whose wampum of peace is a bow in the sky, and believed he would take him to an immortal hunting ground where the paleface would not molest him nor game disappear.

The Christian adores the God who created the heavens and earth and all they contain, and follows a faith that teaches them to live in bonds of friendship with all mankind and dies with hope of bliss beyond the grave.

While the big fool takes God's holy name upon his lips, every action belies his word. He fears no god nor serves none. He profanes His holy name and treats Him as he would not dare to treat an earthly ruler whose power to punish is not to be compared to His, forgetting that every oath is a prayer; prayers that they would not wish to have answered, yet God does sometimes answer them with a vengeance. Last fourth of July some men who had spent the day in drinking in an adjoining town and went to the home of one of their companions, who lived alone and was the most intoxicated of them, threw himself on his bed and was soon in a drunken slumber. The rest proposed to have a prayer meeting and prayed that the Lord would take home their host as they had no more use for him. Sometime after they went to the bed and found God had answered their prayer, for he was dead. They rushed out in great fright and alarmed the neighbors. God had only answered their prayer. They found to their sorrow that God does answer prayer, as millions of others will when it will be too late to take them back. You are too wise to be caught in the gospel trap while you are already in the coils of the devil's net. You boast of your liberty while you are a slave to your passions, avarice and pride. You forfeit the privileges of reigning on a throne with Christ and accept in lieu of it one in partnership with the devil and his eternal punishment for the sake of trying to enjoy some of the miseries of this present life. While you deny and defy the great God of love and mercy you have a god whom you honor and adore; yes, and bow down to, in the very dust. He is on your mind when you lie down to sleep and when you wake in the morning. You give him your money, your strength; yes, and your life. Yet you are so much ashamed of him that you never speak of him in public. Do you want to know who he is? I will let Saint Paul tell you and to what he will lead you. " Whose end is destruction; whose god is their belly, and whose glory is in their shame, who mind earthly things." He also tells what will become of your god as well as its worshipers. " Meat for the belly and the belly for meat, but God will destroy both it and them. For the body is not for fornication but for the Lord, and the Lord for the body." Your god will not aid you when you come in the great tribulation, for that kind of meat will not take the place of the bread of life. I adjure you in the name of the living God to flee from these things and give yourself unreservedly to the living God that you may be able to escape those things that shall come to all that dwell on the earth and stand before the Son of God. Do not say, I am unworthy, and the great theologians are pressing in and blocking up the way; for what Christ said to the chief priests and elders is as true to-day: " Verily I say unto you that the publicans and harlots go into the kingdom of God before you." So I say unto you be a fool no longer but accept the wisdom of the wise.

The second class are those who are wise in their own conceit. They have graduated from their denominational college and have learned to twist the Bible so it fits in their creed as perfectly as does a duck's foot in the mud. They have their church history at their tongue's end and can give the history of all their great men from Wesley, Calvin, Fox or Luther down to Sam Jones. But if you ask them about Wesley's quarrel with Whitefield and driving him out of London, or Calvin's persecuting Servatus to the stake, or Fox's quarrel with Bunyan, or Luther's retiring from his great work and becoming irritable and vulgar at the age of 40, you will find them in blissful ignorance. I spoke of his retirement to a Lutheran minister, who made a great display of his learning and could read the New Testament in seven different languages. He said he had never heard of it before and supposed he had prosecuted his work until the day of his death, nor had he ever heard of his quarrel with Erasmus, his former co-worker, of which his biographer says: "In the vehemence of his hostility to the doctrine of Erasmus, Luther was led into various assertions of a very questionable kind, besides in indulging in very wild abuse of his opponent's character;" and adds the quarrel was a very unhappy one. Strange! Who can tell what kinds of quarrels are happy ones? The dispute grew over Erasmus saying Christ was the Son of God eternal; while Luther said he was the eternal Son of God. I do not pretend to be theologian enough to tell which is wrong, for to me they appear both right, as there is about as much difference as there is between tweedledum and tweedledee.

It is not my purpose to malign these men who have in the providence of God brought about great reforms, but to show what broken sticks men are to lean on since the mystery of perfection was lost. If the student will carefully study the life of Luther he will be able to see the stone over which he stumbled and why he spent his last twenty years in idleness; but his fall was the means of bringing the church half way out of the pit into which it had fallen. Its full restitution is just before us, but the wise fools think they have all of the truth and a little more. I lately heard a minister preach that Paul, if here to-day and preached as he did, would be considered an old fogy, as in this advanced age religion had advanced with the times and the gospel preached by Christ and the Apostles was not in keeping with the theology of to-day. I do not know but some of the wise fools have got ahead of God, and my advice would be for them to wait and give Him a chance to catch up. I asked a Presbyterian minister who believed in final perseverance to explain to me Hebrews, 6: 1 to 8. He said the Apostle presumed a case that could not exist. So you see they always have a hole to crawl out of. The colored preacher was telling about God's making Adam out of clay and stood him against the fence to dry, when a "brudder" arose in the back part of the room and asked, "Who made de fence?" "You shut up back dare or you will upset all our theology."

If you go to one of the wise ones and tell him you want to learn his theology, swallow down all he chooses to feed you, like a chicken does corn, without asking any whys and wherefores, you would be considered very wise, but do not ask them for their proof nor try to teach them anything, or they will say: "The idea of your coming here to teach us," as I was told once down in Jersey. I was sent by the Lord to tell Dr. A. B. Simpson something and asked for fifteen minutes' conversation, and waited before his door a whole week, but he kept putting it off until I left him in disgust. The truth was I wanted to tell him something, and as he knew all about the Bible and his Antichrist there was no room for more, when the poor fool did not know the way into Christ's kingdom. If I had come to learn about his Antichrist or how he lost the gift of healing the sick he would have wasted lots of time on me.

All of the wise ones do not fill the pulpits, or rather occupy them, but you will find them in the pew and they have their creed well learned and are ready with an answer, but if you ask such questions as, Could God have saved the world without the sacrifice of his son? Or, how are we accountable for Adam's sin? Or, how are we benefitted by the cross of Christ? They will say, "I will run and ask the dominie," and when he returns he will say, "These questions are not important, and all that is necessary is in the catechism." That is, where ignorance is bliss it is folly to be wise, and a little learning is a dangerous thing; but when they find themselves shut out of the kingdom in the tribulation they will find that their blissful ignorance was folly personified.

To these wise ones I would say get the Holy Spirit and put a loose rein on your creeds and churchism and let the spirit of truth lead you into all truth and then you will know just how much truth and how much error there is in your church, and you will get a peace that is above all worldly peace; but trust in no man, and if any man seemeth to be wise, let him become a fool that he may be wise.

The third class are like Paul, who was a fool for Christ's sake. This is by far the most important class of fools, as they are very foolish and despised by the world but very much honored by God.

A lady had a foolish son and as she had some strangers at dinner she told him not to say anything and they would not find out he was a fool. One said, "Sonny, what is your name?" No answer. Another, "How old are you?" Another, "Do you go to school?" Why the boy is a fool! Then he said, whimpering: "Its no use mother, they found out that I was a fool and I never said a word."

The Lord's fools have not had better success. I know a Catholic who was converted and tried to keep his religion to himself and in a short time he had no religion to keep. So he started the second time with so much zeal that he was sure that he could convert his parents, and was successful—in getting turned out of doors.

The choice is now between the kingdom and the great tribulation, and the contrast is so great that there is no comparison between them. Nominal

Christianity will not save us. We must lay aside every weight and we must strain every nerve for the fight and with a determination to get there, and success is certain if we do not waiver. It is now hardly necessary to count the cost. If we have property in the war we cannot save it from the great conflagration. Tradition says the rich young man who came to Christ and was asked to sell all and follow Him, lost his property when Jerusalem was taken and burned. What will your mortgages be worth when the cities of the nations fall by the great earthquake and the hills and mountains cast into the sea, or your bank stock when the safes melt in the great heat. But we look for a new heaven and a new earth wherein dwelleth righteousness. So we can afford to let the fools laugh at us for the time will soon come when it will be our turn to laugh, and then we, the sons of God, will shout for joy, and we shall be able to keep it up for a thousand years, while those who now laugh will weep and lament while we rejoice, for then they will learn that they who laugh last laugh best.

Prepare for a greater sacrifice than the churches have asked you to make, for as James says, " Humble yourself before the mighty hand of God and He will lift you up;" for we cannot make any sacrifice for God but what he is able and willing to return a hundred fold.

Let the man who would be wise remember that the wisdom of the world is foolishness with God, so what he can learn of human teachers will be to him of but little value, for all true spiritual wisdom must come from God through the spirit, and the fear of God is the beginning of wisdom, and the true student will tremble at His word, while the wise fool who would instruct him has no great fear of his inferior. So the most important thing a man can learn is that he is a fool, for then he will see the necessity of a true teacher. The wise man says, "Seeth thou a man wise in his own conceit, there is more hope of a fool than of him." When the spirit led me into the most important truth I wrote my experience to a friend, now a Ph. D., who wrote back he believed it a device of Satan, but when the same spirit led him into the same he wrote: "What fools we are anyhow, for when we think we know something we know nothing as we ought to know it." I do not apply this to you but to myself.

I heard Rev. Stephen Merritt tell the following when he was Grand Worthy Patriarch of the Sons of Temperance. He was invited to give a lecture in the central part of the State. Two men were delegated to meet him at the station who did not know him, and as other strangers left the train they were puzzled to tell which was him, so they approached one and asked him if he was the Grand Worthy Patriarch. He said, "The grand what? What do you take me for? I am nothing of the kind." Then they approached another with the same result, while Merritt was enjoying the joke, as, he like Paul, is a short man of not very prepossessing appearance. Then they shouted, hello, when he came forward and they put the question to him, and he said he was. They said: "What! You?" Man looketh on the outward appearance.

SEVENTEENTH STEP.

The Church of Rome.

"Thus saith the Lord, cursed in the man that trusteth in man and maketh flesh his arm."—Jer. 17: 5.

The Church of Rome taught, when their church ruled the world, that there was no salvation outside of their church, so kings would rather resign their crown than fall under the ban of the Pope. But since the reformation such men as George Muller, D. L. Moody, Whitefield, Wesley, Spurgeon, and an army of others, have given unmistakable evidence that God has not confined his blessing to the Catholic. But their ministers still teach that they are the original and only true church and all Protestants are guilty of heresy. Do they believe it? If they did, I believe what I now relate would be impossible.

After serving as priest 12 years, Rev. James A. O'Connor, of 142 West 21st Street, New York, editor of the Converted Catholic, became convinced of its error, left that church, and has for 21 years devoted his life to convincing Catholics of the error of the church. As a result he has taken 65 priests by the hand and led them out of the Catholic church. If they knew that their church was the true one this would be impossible, for he is by no means an orator, but convinces by plain statement of facts. If the stories he tells about the priests and bishops are true, they are far from being saved men, and if they are not true the priests would know it and he would have no influence over them. But they that he has brought out confirm his report. When he takes a priest out of the Catholic church he takes him from a good living (for no church feeds them as well, for the Catholic parsonage here is the finest and best kept of any in this place, and the former priest boasted of having the fastest trotting horse in the town) and had nothing to give in return but the sure hope of salvation. I heard him say a few years ago that a priest had just told him he would leave his church if he would insure him a living. But he replied he had to trust the Lord for his own.

At O'Connor's 21st anniversary of his work he held a convention, where many of the converted priests took a part, among which was Rev. Dr. D. F. McFaul, who was 10 years a Catholic priest, but was converted by O'Connor's ministry. I give an extract from his speech: "After years of meditation I concluded that my soul could not fly upward on a creed of forms and ceremonies, juggleries and incantations. I lost faith in my ability to change wafers into the identical flesh and wine, and water into the blood of our Lord Jesus Christ. I could not change these elements into the 'body and blood,' the 'soul and divinity' of the son of God, as the Romans falsely teach. I lost faith in transubstantiation. I lost faith in my ability to absolve the sinner from his sins against God. I realized that I could not save in being occupied with these accessories that the Church of Rome uses so much—masses and indulgences, holy water, relics, etc., and I felt that the poor people were imposed upon and deprived of their money by extortion. I felt, too, that they received no adequate benefit for the money paid to me and to other priests for ceremonies and sacraments. My soul sickened at the thought of receiving money for dragging souls out of purgatory. It became so offensive to me that I could no longer endure to stay amid the corruptions and abominations of the old church. My eldest brother promised me any amount of money if I would only stay and 'go with the crowd,' as he said. I had money in every pocket then. I had horses and carriages, riches and the approbation of the people. But I thank God that in giving up all these things I have something much better—the peace of God that passes all understanding.

"I would to God that all Catholics would leave their priests, their bishops and the Pope and come out on the Lord's side. Then they would give up all bad habits and become children of God. How much less drunkenness there would be in the world, how much less would be the number of souls lost if Roman Catholics were only truly converted. Nine-tenths of the rumsellers are Catholics, and they will not abandon their nefarious business until they become Christians. I would to God they understood what conversion is! I would not hesitate to promise a large sum of money to any Roman Catholic who would point to me the hour and place where he was converted and experienced a change of heart. I am not afraid I would have to pay the money, for unfortunately they know nothing of real conversion, they know nothing of redemption, they know nothing of real salvation. The only conversion that they know, the only way to become a christian which they know, is by the water of baptism being sprinkled on the head of an infant child. . I know by my own experience that although I had plenty of money as a priest, and everything that the world could give me, I had not the peace of God. I sighed by day and groaned by night until God spoke peace to my soul. I consider it idolatry when they kneel to a pure wafer of bread, believing the priest has power to change the bread into the body and blood of Christ and adore that as God. I, myself, created

God out of water and was then oblige to eat it. Think of a human being creating his God and then eating him.

"Unfortunately the habit of drinking liquor is not confined to the laity; the clergy also indulge to excess. I remember on one occasion when a bishop was buried, how the event was celebrated by the consumption of a large quantity of intoxicants. Many of the clergy put up at a prominent hotel, where there was great revelry during the night. When the servants cleaned out the room next morning there was a fearful revelation of the carousing that had taken place. A large number of empty bottles were placed outside the rooms occupied by the priests, and the waiters complained that they had never been so taxed in all their lives as during that night, carrying champagne and whiskey to their clerical guests."

Dr. McFraul has been a Methodist minister for 18 years.

I heard O'Connor say the priests drink to excess, but do not blame them, for they do it to smother the conviction that they are deceiving the people. While he has been taking out 65 priests from the Roman Catholic Church he has taken out about 10,000 laymen.

I once had the care of 30 fresh air children that were picked up in the streets of New York, most of which were Catholics, and found that nearly all of their homes were without Bibles. So I went to a Catholic bookstore and tried to buy Catholic Bibles for them. They had not a Bible in the store. So I asked them to find if they could get them. I feared their parents would take offense if I gave them Protestant ones. The bookseller doubtless consulted the priest, and when I called again they said there were no Catholic Bibles published but large ones, that cost $12 each, which was a Catholic lie, for I ordered for myself through a Protestant bookseller one for $1, no better than the Bible Society sells for 20 cents. Then I purchased Protestant Bibles for them. Before the reformation it was a sin against the holy inquisition to be found with a Bible, and only a few years ago Spain imprisoned its subjects and banished foreign missionaries for circulating Bibles.

Why do they not want their members to have Bibles? Because they would find that the doctrine of Rome contradicts the teachings of the Bible; for they find no purgatory, holy water, consecrated burial ground, infant baptism, prayer to Mary and the Saint, or confessing and receiving absolution from the priests in the Bible. In short if they would get it and compare it with the teachings of their church they would cease to be Catholics. Since Protestants circulate Bibles they allow but not encourage them to buy Bibles, but sell them at a high price; the profit goes to the church. I am told that when they get one they send for the priest, who blesses it and closes it, after which they dare not open it.

I asked an orphan if she prayed. She said she prayed to the Virgin Mary every night and morning. I asked her if she prayed to her father. She said, no, for he was dead and could not hear her. I told her that the Virgin Mary was dead and had been for 1800 years, and could not hear her any more than her father could, for the Bible says that the dead know nothing at all.

If there is any blessing to be obtained in this or the future life we owe it to our mother, who is, under God, the author of our existence, for without her we could not have had an existence. But Christ was under no such obligation to the Virgin Mary, for he had a being thousands of years before she ever lived, and he was Divine or God, while she was carnal, of the seed of fallen Adam, and God used her to degrade the Son from the divine to the state of fallen man, which subjected him to the degradation of the death on the cross that he might teach men the way to return to God. Instead of her having any influence or power over her son she had to look to him for her own salvation, and never during his ministry did he recognize or call her mother, and when told that his mother was without he said his disciples were his mother, ignoring her claim. After her brief life she died and was buried and will remain in the grave until the resurrection day. So who will hear or record or answer all of these prayers offered to her? Surely she cannot, and it is no better than praying to an idol.

I have yet to learn of a Catholic who dies happy. Before my sister died she was so anxious to be with Jesus that she could hardly wait for her appointed time. She saw heaven open and Jesus with outstretched arms to receive her. She chose for her funeral text, "To die is gain." Show me a Catholic with such an experience. When they are dying they send for the priest, vainly hoping they can help them through for which they have no Scripture. Cardinal Gibbon, who died in England in 1891, spent his last conscious breath praying for mercy, without any evidence that it was answered. Father McGlynn died recently in Newburgh with the same experience. Christians die happy praising the Lord. I visited the deathbed of an old man, and asked if I should pray with him, but my prayer was interrupted by his shouting praises to God. He greatly rejoiced when he was told that he could not recover. Tell me of a Catholic who had such an experience.

EIGHTEENTH STEP.

War.

From whence came wars and fightings among you? Came they not hence even of your lust that war in your members?—James 4: 1.

Had man remained in his primitive state and had he not sinned, for which part of the punishment was death, death would have been an impossibility. In answer to the argument that men would be killed by accident I reply that God never met with a fatal accident, neither will those who fully obey and trust him. He who can save from the fiery furnace, the lion's mouth and the boiling oil, can save in any other emergency. They can tread on serpents, and if they drink any deadly thing it will not hurt them. He will give his angels charge concerning thee, to keep thee in all thy ways, lest thou dash thy foot against a stone. They argue that God directed his people to exterminate their enemies by war and he even fought with them. Certainly under the old law, because Adam's sin reversed the human heart and gave man anger, enmity, hatred and strife, in the place of love, peace and fellowship, and God knew it was impossible for them with their fallen nature to love their enemies; so he gave a law that accorded with their nature, which was love your friends and hate your enemies. An eye for an eye, a tooth for a tooth, and life for life, which does not seem to be a hard law for the most ungodly to keep. But when Christ came he told us how we could change our nature or hearts so it would be as easy to keep his law, which says: Love your enemies, do good to them that despitefully use and persecute you, love and hate not. If thine enemy hunger, feed him (while in war they try to starve him); if he thirsts give him drnk (while down in Cuba they stop up their wells during the hot season).

The question is, are the so called Christian nations living under and fulfilling the law of Moses or the gospel of Christ? All must agree that while they are Chris'ian in name they are Jews by nature and precept. I firmly declare that no spiritual Christian can under any pertext take the life of his fellow, and self defence is no excuse. Christ says: "If any one smite thee on one cheek turn to him the other also." If it was not so pitiable it would be amusing to see how some try to carry out the letter without the spirit. A Quaker fulfilled the law just quoted and then turned on his assailant and whipped him. Another did better who captured a burglar in his house loaded with his goods and instead of turning him over to the law got him on his knees and prayed for him until he was converted, and he became a preacher. Another saw a little girl stealing his pears and he took her a basketful every day until they were gone. If they take thy coat give them thy cloak also. Of all the religious sects I know of I find the Quakers come the nearest to the fulfillment of Christ's teachings. What will I do if I am drafted? The Quakers will answer that question, for they have refused to fight for over 200 years, and if compelled to go to the front refuse to carry or fire a gun, and the nations finally allowed them to remain unmolested at home. Suppose some one seeks to take my life and I can prevent it by taking his? Do not do it, for a man who would take your life is not prepared to die and needs time to repent, while you say with Paul, I prefer to be with Christ, which is far better. (I am talking to Christians.)

But I have a wife and family that needs my support? Christ can take better care of them than you can. So your enemy may have and you should love our neighbor as yourself and seek not your own but your neighbor's wealth. But some wars are necessary. Spain should have been compelled to pay for the blowing up of the Maine which caused the death of so many of our soldiers; should it not? That would not have been seeking your neighbor's wealth, for out of one blood God created all nations. How many of those who perished with the Maine did Admiral Dewey restore to life by sinking the Spanish fleet with so much human life? Do you think the angels before the throne rejoiced over Dewey's victory? Is not the man who can make the most widows and orphans the most honored of men? It reminds me of the boys who were killing frogs and said it is fun for us but it is death to you. It is sad to think that our whole nation from the most saintly D. D. to the lowest criminal rejoice at what they call a great victory, when it only means so many new made graves, so many new made widows and orphans, so much territory wrested from one owner and given to another. Our nation wants Spain to turn over a thousand or two of its rich, productive islands that we have wrested from her. I think it is as unreasonable as it would be for a burglar to rob a bank and then present a bill of charges to pay him for cracking the safe. I have no doubt that Spain would have been glad to have sold Cuba, and that for much less than the war has cost, and then if we wished to be liberal we could have given the Cubans their independence and stopped the effusion of blood, for human life is not to be compared to dollars and cents; but there was too much of the Cain spirit to admit of any forgiveness, forgetting that vengeance belongs to God. Christ said, " Fear not them that kill the body." The Christian martyrs are the only ones that will wear the triple crown; the called, the chosen and the faithful; called by water, chosen by blood, and faithful in martyrdom, and will occupy the best places in Christ's kingdom. But none that fall in war will wear it, for Christ summed up the subject in one sentence: "They that use the sword shall perish by the sword." By this he did not mean temporal, but spiritual death. The faith we follow teaches us to live in bonds of friendship with all mankind and die with hope of bliss beyond the grave.

The history of the world is a history of war, rapine, murder and suffering. The poet truly says, man's inhumanity to man makes countless thousands mourn. The entire population of the globe would come far short of filling the places of those that have fallen in battle in the world's history. In the so called holy wars the pretended Christians have out done far for murder and rapine the most brutish savage.

In A. D. 635 Jerusalem was besieged and captured by the Mohammedan, Calif Omar, who built on the site of the Jewish Temple the mosque of Omar, which remains there to-day. A portion of the inhabitants he compelled to pay a ransom for their freedom, and liberated thousands who were too poor to pay it, but granted life to all, and Christians were allowed to go there on pilgrimage. In the closing years of the eleventh century an uncouth, short man, wearing a single garment with a huge cross upon his back, barehead and barefoot, was riding an ass through Europe. It was Peter the Hermit, who had visited the Holy Land and found the holy sepulcher in the hands of the infidels, and told his story with so much eloquence and feeling, for his tears were more eloquent than his words, that all Europe flocked under his standard, and he got a decree from the Pope that all that went would be absolved from all the sins that they had or would commit, and all that fell in the war would be translated directly to glory. They all wore a red cross sewed on their back or shoulder. A division of the army of 50,000 were defeated by the Mohammedans long before they got there and were nearly annihilated, but there was enough left to take the city after they had taken Cesarea. After Jerusalem had surrendered these holy Christian warriors wearing the cross put 60,000 Jews and Mohammedans to the sword, or murdered them in cold blood. This was in 1099. Eighty-eight years later it again fell into the hands of the Mohammedans, who took it without unnecessary bloodshed and they have held it nearly ever since, showing the Mohammedans are more humane than the Christians.

In less than a century after Luther freed Germany of the thraldom of the Pope, the Emperor tried to restore it by annihilating the Lutherans, for it is said he would rather reign over a barren waste than over protestantism and commenced the 30 years religious (?) war, in which over 10,000,000 perished, and at its close their population was reduced ten millions and real estate was worth less than one-fourth of what it was when it commenced, and it closed because there was neither money nor food to carry it farther, as famine had visited them and men sought their fellow man so they could kill them and eat them. So they signed the peace at Westphalia which gave equal liberty to all, but when the infallible Pope heard of it he had not got his fill of blood and refused to accept it and wanted them to re-open the war. To recover the loss the Emperor compelled all priests to marry and allowed other men to take two wives each. But why repeat these horrors of war. If you want more read the massacre of the Hugenots of France, or of the Protestants in Ireland, or the Reign of Terror in Paris.

If God permits us to punish Spain, the country of the Holy (?) Inquisition, in which 20,000 perished at the stake under one man's rule, let us be careful that we do not do it too well, for God used the heathens to punish the Jews and afterwards punished them for it and even punished others who rejoiced at their misfortunes. Afflictions must come, but woe unto them by whom they come. Peace societies and congresses have little influence when nations get angry. Wars will come. Antichrist will soon deluge the world in war, but let Christians stand aloof. During Christ's millennial reign there will be universal peace for the advocates of peace. But after the thousand years will occur the greatest battle in the world's history.

Russia has led in holding a great international peace congress in Holland, which is well, but let Russia learn a lesson for herself by living in peace with her own peaceful, law-abiding subjects; let her recall her banished Scavis, a band that lived the nearest to the truth as taught by Christ of any church on earth. Their only offence was they believed the bible. But of all Russia's inconsistencies the banishment of some 10,000 of its best and most industrious citizens, who were expelled last winter to come to Canada. Their only offence against the government was that they will not take the oath to go to war. They permitted them to go on conditions that they never return. They are called Dunkhobors. Here is a nation that poses before the nations as universal peace teachers and expels from its own land forever those who accept Christ's precepts of peace. Are we to understand that Russia's recent peace movement is only to disarm other nations so they can make them an easy prey? If their principles were to apply to themselves they would not drive them away who accepted their own teachings. O, consistency, thou art a jewel. It sounds like crying peace when there is no peace; but like all peace movements that is not begotten by the Prince of Peace. The very nations that are crying peace are straining every nerve to increase their armament. Did the United States talk about peace or arbitration after the Maine was blown up? They said to the nations, " Hands off." Does France ask for help to settle their Dreyfus trouble? In times of peace it is easy to raise a cry of peace, but when a nation is angry they will none of it. Unless peace is implanted in the soul by the Holy Spirit it will not avail. If we do not accept it we will have no part in Christ's millennial reign. Let us have peace.

NINETEENTH STEP.

Christ in Politics.

Render unto Caesar the things that are Caesars.

The only part that the people had to take in politics in Christ's day was to obey the laws and pay their taxes, and the words of the text referred to the latter only. During the 450 years of the Judges the people had little or nothing to say about the appointment of their rulers, for they were selected by God. God also appointed their kings. But the throne we honor is our people's choice, says the politician; but a republican form of government is moral or religious so far as the majority of the citizens are moral or religious, and I think a census of our nation would reveal more voters that swear than that pray, so we cannot be called a Christian nation, although many religious professors vote and get into office. But the question the Christian should ask is, if Christ was in my place what would He do? Remember when we vote for a man he becomes our servant and we are morally responsible for all of his official acts, for we have bid him God-speed, which is a greater responsibility than we are willing to accept. But who can deny the fact that those who elected the present government are responsible for the evils and casualties of the late and present war which we bought for twenty millions of dollars, to say nothing of the cost and casualties of the insurrection. What are Christians to do, remain at home on election days and let the sinners run the government? As long as the sinners are in the majority I think they will run it in spite of the Christians and they might as well stay away as vote. Those who support the government are responsible for the annual deaths of nearly one hundred thousand that fill drunkards' graves. Of all of the political parties seeking power the Prohibitionists would give the best rule, but as the best men are the fewest there are not enough of them to make a plurality over any of the other great parties because people think more of their appetites than they do their own or neighbors' health, wealth or happiness. If they could vote the saloon closed to their neighbors and open for themselves I think the Prohibitionists would get more votes. If there was a prospect of the Prohibitionists coming into power a lot of office seekers would flock into the party whose highest ambition would be the spoils of office or big pay for little or no work, and if they fail to obtain it will soon leave the party. If the party in power has to represent a majority of the voters, which are sinners, the Christian does not want to be unequally yoked together with unbelievers. Neither is he a sojourner, but a pilgrim seeking a better country and would not be expected to try to rule the country their pilgrimage takes them through. Christ did not dictate to Herod what laws he should make, nor did He make any effort to get John released from his unjust imprisonment. Our duty is to get ourselves and neighbors to meet Christ at his coming and that will require all of our time and attention. A man that is going to be a soldier does not entangle himself with the affairs of this life that he might please him that has called him to be a soldier. The prince of this world is the devil, who is now ruling through his faithful agents and will soon rule in person. It is well to pray for rulers and ask for them to be kept as much as possible from Satan's power, but be mindful that the worst government the world has ever seen is soon to come and the sooner the better, for then we will know that the day of our redemption draweth near. But who wants to help Satan run his government? The Christian will not accept any political office or meddle with politics, but keep himself pure for Christ's sake; but when the world is made new and Christ comes to reign over it he will be invited to share the kingdom with Him who did not die to save the nation but the individual.

TWENTIETH STEP.

Money and Religion.

It is easier for a camel to go through the eye of a needle than for a rich man to enter into the kingdom of God—Mat. 19: 24.

Many try to explain the text by saying there was a gate through the wall of Jerusalem just large enough to let a camel squeeze through that was called the needle's eye; but I cannot find any such gate on the maps of ancient Jerusalem nor any authentic description of it. If there was such a gate then all camels could get through and all rich men into the kingdom and Christ would have said the needle's eye instead of the eye of a needle and prove Christ in error when he said, "Unless a man forsaketh all that he hath he cannot be my disciple." We must remember the difference between being saved and in the kingdom, which none but disciples can inherit. Christ said, "Go ye into all the world and disciple all nations." Anyone can be a disciple that will pay the price. If we love our neighbor as ourselves we will want him to live in as good a house and have all the comforts of life that we do, and if we divided with every poor family we met we would soon be as poor as they. Would Christ hoard up money as long as heathens are dying in darkness for the want of means to send them the light? Christ did not say sell a tenth or fourth or half, but all that thou hast and give alms and take up thy cross and follow me.

A merchant who had prospered and lived in the old

home, which was very humble, concluded he could afford a better one, so he built one that corresponded with his improved circumstances. When it was completed a neighbor said he was suited with it and asked him to sell it to him. He replied that he built it for himself and would not sell; and moved into it. At the first family altar he read, "The foxes have holes, the birds of the air have nests, but the son of man hath not where to lay his head." He then said while the Saviour of the world was without a home is it right for me to live in such luxury? "Wife, is not the old house good enough?" She thought so. The neighbor got the house and the price went to help the needy.

To illustrate, suppose John and George go to buy each a suit of clothes. They each have just fifty dollars. The merchant says he has suits from ten dollars up to fifty. Here are some royal suits for fifty dollars. "Have you any cheaper royal suits," says John. "No, but here is an imitation for twenty but it is not nearly as good, will not wear and is easily soiled, and any one can easily detect the difference." "I do not believe in putting my last dollar in a royal robe when I can get one for thirty dollars less, beside Miss World expects me to take her to Vanity's Ball to-night and if I do not I will lose my suit with her, and the imitation is good enough for that, and to spend the night properly will cost ten dollars or more," says John.

But, says George, "The prince has a grand reception to-morrow and all are expected to wear royal apparel." "I will be there, too," says John, "and I guess he cannot detect the imitation, and you would be a fool to beggar yourself for the reception while I can buy lots of vanities for the other thirty dollars." "I will forego the ball for the sake of attending the prince's reception and will buy the royal robes," says George.

So John took Miss World to Vanity's Ball and spent the remaining thirty dollars and got so much intoxicated that Miss World had to get another to escort her home and he soiled his suit. He attempted to attend the reception with his imitation, which was detected at once and he was cast into prison; while George was cordially welcomed. The prince hearing of the sacrifice he made to attend was so well pleased with him that he made him his steward.

Jesus said unto them: "Verily, I say unto you that ye which have followed me, in the generation when the son of man shall sit in the throne of his glory, ye also shall sit upon twelve thrones judging the twelve tribes of Israel."—Matt. 19: 28.

Under the law the Jews were allowed to accumulate wealth and put it to interest or usury to Gentiles only, as they were told to lend to their brethren without interest. After the Babylonian captivity the rulers exacted one per cent. interest, which displeased God, so He visited them with famine, and Nehemiah sharply rebuked them and made them return it.—Nehemiah 5: 6-12.

Nothing is taught in the New Testament about usury, as it was not necessary, for they were taught not to accumulate wealth.

If a brother has money or goods that he has no present use for and another is in need, it is his duty to let him have it, but not to speculate with. If he does not have to pay interest he can return it sooner. But if a man is faithful he will not have to borrow, for our promise of bread and raiment is sure, and the Word says, "Owe no man anything, but to love one another."—Rom. 13: 8.

To run in debt will check the spiritual growth of a person or a church. George Muller, the greatest faith man of the century, fed and housed over a thousand orphans and never borrowed a dollar. Most of the churches are either borrowers or lenders of money on interest. Many receive bequests of money to be invested and the interest used. They ought not to receive such legacies. What will they do with the principal when the world burns? If it is wrong to borrow it is equally so to tempt others to borrow. Suppose Smith, when he commenced life for himself was left by a relative a sufficient sum of money for which he had performed no service, to enable him to launch out into business. Being a shrewd dealer and good manager and having a prudent wife and no more family he soon massed a sufficient fortune to enable him to retire from business. He purchased a house with some of his surplus that he could rent for 15 per cent. per annum of its cost. He is a member of the church and pays a small percent. of his income toward its support. He rents the house to Jones who is a member of the same church, but had not all of these advantages. He was not naturally as good a manager, which was his misfortune but not his fault. He had a large family which to clothe, feed and educate and pay his rent took all of his hard earning, giving him no time for rest nor no hope for it this side of the grave. Smith stands ready each month to take his sweat money, for which he has no need further than to add to his invested horde, and considers it simply a business transaction involving no religious duty. If Jones was sick or in suffering want he would help him, but as long as he is able to earn the rent he sees no reason why he should not pay it. Yet if he loved him as himself he would want Jones to have as much rest as himself and live as comfortably, and if it was impossible or unwarranted to bring him up where he was he should descend where Jones is and take his place in the shop or on the farm to enable him to get some rest. In less than 7 years or 5, if it is invested at the same rate of interest, Jones pays him the price of his house and he has nothing to do but to pay for it again or move out. A Christian way would be for Smith to put the rent to a sinking fund and when he had paid him the cost of the house give him the deed and thus secure for him a home for his declining days and take the money to help some one else in a similar way.

The time is near when a load of gold will not purchase a dinner, and it will be cast into the streets and none will stoop to pick it up.

The rich Russian, Count Tolstoi, has the correct opinion. He has laid aside his rich clothes and donned peasants' garb, and takes his place in the field and works with them and has discharged the servants that formerly waited on him, and has given away most of his wealth. He was founder of the recent peace congress.

Getting up entertainments to draw money from sinners to support churches is unchristian and unscriptural. God will not accept anything from the sinner before the heart is given. "Thy prayers and thine alms," says God. Quite a controversy is going on in the Christian Herald as to whether a church should accept money offered by a liquor seller. I say if the money is offered unsolicited without specification, accept it, but tell him it will not purchase his salvation. Spurgeon said when he commenced preaching he was in need of a hat and asked the Lord to send the means. A miser called him aside and put a half crown in his hand, saying the Lord directed him to give. It was enough to get the hat. Awhile later he gave him another half, saying the Lord told him to give him a crown but thought a half would do, and asked him to pray for him that he might be cured of his covetousness. When he was on his death bed he crawled down stairs so as to die on the first floor and save the shilling the undertaker charged for carrying a corpse down stairs. In this case the Lord directed a sinner to render aid to his servant and of course it was his duty to accept it.

TWENTY-FIRST STEP.

Christian Perfection.

"Ye are gods. If ye call them gods unto whom the word of God came, and the Scripture cannot be broken."—John 10: 34-35.

Hark! Do I not hear you all say I have heard enough on that subject, give us something new? They all turned out to hear the new minister's first sermon, and remarked, "He is smart and has given us a rousing sermon on repentance. If he keeps it up he will fill the house." The next Lord's Day they all went to hear the next subject, but they were not so well pleased, for he took the same text and preached nearly the same sermon, and it was the same the third week. Then a committee waited on him and asked if that was all the sermons he had. He said he had more when they were ready for them, but the first thing for them to do was to repent, and he had told them to do so three times but they had not done it, but when they did he would tell them what to do next. I propose to preach perfection until you are perfect, then we will change the subject.

Do you call it sacrilege to call men gods? If so, Christ taught sacrilege, for I have quoted His words, and I am not afraid to preach anything I find in the Bible. An eminent theologian says that after man had transgressed His law He could have left him to eternal condemnation without providing any way of salvation without any injustice to himself. That might read well in poetry but it is not true. The sinner may have the choice of a dozen different roads to go, but the perfect man has but one, and he is so perfectly led by the spirit that the way is always plain before him. It is so with the perfect God. He created a perfect man to serve Him. Then He created the tempter to deceive and draw him away. I ask any intelligent person if He could have left him to utter destruction without providing any way for escape and still be a God of love and mercy? Would it not be judgment without mercy, like many laws of sinful men? Here is a case in point: A murderer had bitterly repented and became a Christian and sent for the Christian wife of the man he had slain that he might ask her pardon for the great wrong he had done, which was freely granted. Yet the rigorous law said he must suffer the death penalty. While God says of the penitent man: "His sins and iniquities will I remember no more," and he is the same in God's sight as if he had never sinned. Here we see the contrast between divine and human law. The one is to the penitent, mercy without judgment, the other judgment without mercy. Which do you like best? The Governor has the power to grant to a condemned criminal unconditional pardon, which gives him every political right that he had before he broke the law. I now ask if God is not able to grant the same liberty to His penitent subjects who have once broken His law; or is man more merciful than God? Paul says in Adam all died and in Christ are all made alive. The question is did the resurrection through Christ restore what we lost in Adam? I answer much more. For we are not only restored to Adam's original nature but much more, for Adam never was called a god, or was a partaker of the divine nature. Peter says: "Whereby are given unto us exceeding great and precious promises; that by these ye might be partakers of the divine nature, having escaped the corruption (death) that is in the world through lust." Paul says of Christ: "Being in the form of God, thought it is not robbery to be equal with God; but made himself of no reputation but took upon him the form of a servant and was made in the likeness of man." Christ did not humble himself to save men only because men were both saved and translated before he came and suffered, but it was to exalt us and enable us to partake of His divine nature that we might share both His holiness and power, or in other words, He became man that we could become gods.

An eminent physician, who is not eminent for his piety, for he claimed to be a Unitarian, told me that Christ's life was a perfect example and if we followed it we would be saved, but we gained nothing by his death, and if he had ascended without dying he would have accomplished all that he did. He was much nearer right than modern theologians give him credit of being. I told him he was right in saying if we follow Christ's life and teaching we should surely be saved and become subjects in his kingdom, and that is as far as the modern church gets, as they claim to receive a benefit from Christ's death and receive none, for they refuse to take part in his sufferings and deceive both themselves and their hearers, or as the Apostle says: "Deceiving and being deceived." While the doctor neither deceives himself nor any one else, and I told him we are saved by His life and crowned kings by His death, if we partake of His sufferings.

I recently heard a sermon on faith in prayer. The preacher said if we drew a check on a bank the money had to come if we had an account to our credit in the bank, and if they were unable to honor the check we could close the doors of the bank and they could do no more business. Then he assumed that all Christians had an inexhaustible surplus to draw from in God's bank if they had faith, and told them to draw largely. Suppose I see Levi P. Morton present a check for a thousand dollars and draw the money, so I make one like it only substitute my name instead of his, would I get the money or a protest? They would say you have no credit here so we had to protest, as you must deposit before you can draw. So I say I lacked faith and now I am going to believe I have a credit there and exercise a great deal of faith nothwithstanding the facts of the case. My faith would avail me nothing, for "faith is dead without works." Then I make another check and put Morton's name on it saying then I will surely get the money for he has unlimited credit. But instead of the money I geat a warrant of arrest for forgery. Will those who presume to draw on Christ's righteousness succeed better? A man who believed in faith prayed for the Lord to take a neighbor who had offended him out of his way that night, but there must have been a slight doubt in his mind, for he went the next morning to see if he was yet living, and the facts did not increase his faith, for he was not as successful as the drunken sinners were.

Suppose then as I find a deposit must be made, I deposit one hundred dollars and draw a check for a thousands, would I be more successful? They would tell me if I wished to draw largely I must deposit largely. Yet many work or try to work the Lord's bank on that plan, and are like the man who dropped a nickel in the contribution box and took out a dime in the way of change. Some have been able to draw large sums without making any deposit, like Baker and Seeley did on the Shoe and Leather Bank, but they generally come to grief, as they did. But that game never worked with the Lord's bank, for He employs none but honest bookkeepers who, like Caesar's wife, is above suspicion.

But the trouble is the average churchmember refuses to make any deposit in the Lord's bank. I just asked a lady who strains at a gnat in some matters and spoke reprovingly, too, because I followed the Bible too closely, if she ever gave up anything in her whole life that was a sacrifice, for Christ's sake, and she was unable to answer. She said she had asked the Lord to tell her if it was His will to give up certain things that were forbidden in the Bible but got no answer, but refuses to seek the indwelling Comforter that would teach her the very thing she asks and refuses to follow the teachings she receives.

One night last fall she dreamed she was trying to kill a very fat, but not very long, snake, with a stick; it had two heads and I was trying to hold it for her, but if I held one head it would hiss at me with the other, while she pounded it with a stick. She had an iron in her hand and thought if she got that on it she could kill it, but did not then. I tried to hold it by the tail, but it got away, but got very lean and small by the whipping. But the first thing she did when she got up was to give it a fat breakfast. The snake was her passionate disposition. I had come home late the night before with a wagon after a long drive with some goods to be unloaded in the house, so I left the wagon in the front yard, which was against her orders, expecting to draw it to the side of the house, where we kept it, before she went out; but she went out first and instead of putting it where it belonged, which would have been as easy, she ran it in the middle of the street and said I left it there out of spite. I told her I did not, but asked if she did not run it in the street out of spite. She said, yes. I was mad. I told her the meaning of her dream and said a clean heart was better than a clean dooryard, and fighting the snake was keeping down of passion, and the iron that would have killed it was her iron will, for she is one of those who when she makes up her mind to do a thing, does it, but did not decide to kill the snake, but could make it small by keeping it in check, when her husband pitched in and took her part and hissed at me when I found where the other head was. I think she has fed the snake oftener than she has whipped it, since it has not been reduced in size. The business man who would draw a bank check must deposit largely and keep a large surplus on the credit side; such a man is sure to succeed. It is so with our dealings with the Lord. It was to the Disciples that he said, "Ask anything in my name and I will do it," and they left all to follow him. His last words to them were, "Go ye therefore and make disciples of all nations," but He is not saying that now to us, but He is saying, "make disciples of yourselves." Let us get the beam out of our own eyes first. Since we are required to disciple all nations, as well as ourselves, let us see what deposits in the Lord's bank are required to draw from. Christ said, "Whosoever doth not bear his own cross and come after me cannot be my disciple;" let us make a deposit of that, but we will not find much imputed righteousness in it. Again, "So likewise whosoever he be of you that renounces not all that he hath, cannot be my disciple." You say it costs too much. Yes, it costs something to deposit in the Lord's bank as well as it does in a National bank, but the former will be of very much more service when the world is on fire, for we shall not be able to hire firemen to extinguish the flames with the latter because of the scarcity of water. Christ required three things of the rich young man to make him perfect. First, to sell all that he had and give alms; second, to take up his cross; third, to follow him. I heard a colored minister tell his people that Christ would not allow him to part with his property, but only asked it to try him; but I think He was in the habit of saying what He meant. History says his property was consumed when Jerusalem was burned a few years later and he went into captivity. So he lost both his property, liberty and Christ's kingdom, as I fear many will in this age. But the wise will deposit in Christ's never-failing bank. Again Christ says, "If any man cometh unto me and hateth not his own father, and mother, and wife, and children, and brethren, and sisters, yea and his own life, else also he cannot be my disciple."

I have heard ministers try to explain this away, but it reads the same as it did before. The truth is what the world calls love is the reverse of Christ's love, and is summed up in what I heard a prattling child tell her mother, "I love you tause you love me;" and the world is ready to add, "I hate you because you hate he." None would bestow love upon another unless he though he could get it returned with interest, and when they find no return their love is turned to hate and friendship ends. What wife will not testify to a lie to screen her guilty husband, unless she finds someone that suits her better and sues for a divorce, and then she can lie as comfortable on the other side. I might enlarge on this subject, but not now. How different is christian love that goes out for its enemies and knows no difference.

I was once talking to a convert on the necessity of forgiveness. She said she never would forgive a man, who was a helpless cripple, for he had deeply wronged her, and I need not ask it. A few days later we were in a meeting where the Spirit was doing his work, and as soon as an opportunity was offered she rushed to the cripple and urged him to give himself to the Lord and be healed, and had forgotten her enmity. It is as impossible for the natural man to love his enemies as it is for the spiritual to hate his. The heart that knows no love cannot love and the heart that knows no hatred cannot hate. The truly spiritual man can only see the never dying soul, while the natural can only see the body, and they that are Christ's have crucified the flesh with its passions and lusts. So let us become Christians and lay all narrow, selfish affections on His altar, and let Him in return give us that broad, deep and lofty affection that knows no end and will carry us above all of the fiery trials of this world, and receive the holy spirit and follow Him until He leads us unto Godly perfection and perfect love that casteth out all fear and makes us never dying, God's, and ready to be received when He comes to take up His elect that are to escape the tribulation, and stand before the Son of Man. Even so come Lord Jesus, Amen.

TWENTY-SECOND STEP.

Good Will to Men.

"For the whole law is fulfilled in one word, even in this; thou shalt love thy neighbor as thyself. But if ye hate and devour one another, take heed that ye be not consumed one of another;" Gal. 5, 13-14.

I quote a striking little narrative poem credited to Hunt, containing more truth than fiction.
"Abou Ben Adhem—may his tribe increase—
Awoke one night from a deep dream of peace,
And saw, within the moonlight in his room,
Making it rich and like a lily in bloom,
An angel writing in a book of gold.
Exceeding peace had made Ben Adhem bold,
And to the presence in the room he said:
"What writest thou?" The vision raised his head
And with a look made of all sweet accord,
Answered: "The names of those who love the Lord."
"And is mine one?" said Abou. "Nay, not so,"
Replied the angel. Abou spoke more low
But cheerily still, and said, "I pray thee, then,
Write me as one that loves his fellow-men."
The angel wrote and vanished. The next night
He came again with a great wakening light
And showed the names whom love of God had blest,
And lo! Ben Adhem's name led all the rest."

When we read the law that God gave to Moses and consider the hard and we might say unmerciful judgments in it, and contrast it with the affectionate teachings of Christ, we are apt to look at the

Father as an austere and merciless judge, incapable of love or kindness; while Christ's law of loving precept indicates a nature of the other extreme, or the embodiment of love and mercy. This is very far from the truth, for the two are one in nature and the love of the Father cannot be surpassed by the Son; and He who said an eye for an eye and a tooth for a tooth, and life for life, and said slay your enemies, also said love your enemy and if he smite thee on one cheek turn the other also. God showed as much love and mercy in giving the moral law as he did in Christ's gospel; for the nature of the sin brought into the world by Adam's sin was such as to harden man's heart, so it was impossible for him to love his enemies or to do good to his persecutor. So if God had given the gospel to them before they had received softening power of the Holy Spirit, it would have been impossible for them to have kept it, and no one could have been saved, and would have been unjust to require an impossibility; while the hard law given to Moses was in accord with their hard hearts and made them who obeyed it fit subjects to Christ's kingdom.

The result of man's fall is illustrated in the world's history, which is a record of enemity, hatred, arson and bloodshed, and the country whose history mostly abounds in them we call the most interesting, and the history of the country that runs like this: "The faith we follow teaches us to live in bonds of friendship with all mankind and die in hope of bliss beyond the grave." would be too slow for the modern reader. A minister in speaking of the horrors of war said: " If the inhabitants of the globe were smitten instantly there would not be as many dead unburied as have fallen in war; and the greatest hero has been him who could paint the town reddest with the blood of its citizens." When we pick up the paper we skip the religious news in our eagerness to absorb each line and word of some bloodcurdling murder.

The angels that ushered in the Prince of Peace with "Peace on earth and good will to men," brought in a new state of things and while Christ taught peace he sent the spirit to make it not only passable but natural for us to carry it out, and as a result we have in the New Testament the most loving and peaceable book that the world ever produced, which shows His power to transform a fiend into a friend, as in the case of Paul.

We cannot cultivate a spirit of love for it is God-given, and if the spirit has not planted it in our hearts all love service is vain, "for if I bestow all my goods to feed the poor and give my body to be burned and have not love, it profiteth me nothing," says the Apostle.

When the Spirit was driven from the church in the fourth century, brotherly love took its flight with it. Constantine wrote loving epistles to the contending factions in the church, exhorting them to peace and unity, but to no purpose, for it was crying peace when there was no peace, and the "r" in friend was again dropped and those who called themselves christians took on the nature of wild beasts The Reformation brought in a slight improvement for a time, but soon Protestantism became divided and hatred and discord reigned and brotherly love did not extend beyond its denomination, and now one minister is ready to war with another that comes on what he calls "his field" to get converts. I know a case where a sect had a small organized church, but no house, but held meeting in a school house, and when no meetings had been held there for six months, another minister went and had a revival and organized a little church, which offended the minister who had deserted the field, virtually admitting that they would rather have the sinners lost than have another sect save them. This case is one of many which might be mentioned, but I am happy to say that sectarian prejudice is fast giving way to a better spirit of brotherly love and unity and the way is opening for the great events that are before us. Many have tried to act out the nature of love without the spirit and do it physically, like the Quaker who was smitten on one cheek turned the other and when he received a blow on that turned upon his assailent and gave him a whipping, doubtless with much better grace than he received the blow, which did not manifest much long-suffering, which is the fruit of the spirit; for the fruits of the spirit are love, joy, peace, longsuffering, kindness, goodness, faithfulness, meekness and temperance. Now if any one has the spirit these fruits will be manifest. I have known many who make their boast f the spirit, but failed to produce any of its fruit and were ready to persecute any one who believed more of the Bible than they did. I have learned the hollowness of human friendship. A minister without work or money who was shut up in a distant city with a family without means of getting away, for whom I furnished the means of getting on a field where he could get support, turned against me and refused to do the least favor or give any reason for his lack of brotherhood. I have known them that made a profession of perfection and advertised themselves as Holiness Evangelists and had rare spiritual gifts, become bitter persecuters against even members of their own church, and accepted their teaching because the spirit had led them a step beyond them, which was in accord with His word. I know a case where one was illegally and unconstitutionally imprisoned over a year for accepting some of the plain teachings of Christ, and vainly pleaded with his Holiness brethren (?) for aid when they could have easily have effected his release.

One of the most unbrotherly persecuting and unchristian letters that I ever received was from a man that signed himself Holiness Evangelist, because I sent him my book which reveals the way into the kingdom. I answered, sending stamp, and asked some questions and to return the book, but got neither book nor reply. Even Luther, Calvin, Fox and Wesley are numbered with the persecuters.

It is all because, as I said, we cannot love without the spirit of love and those that have claimed Him have so trammeled Him with their human creeds and teachings that He had no liberty and was driven out.

Many lose Him by refusing to obey, and others fail to get Him for the same reason, which is the sin against the Holy Ghost, for if we refuse to obey Him it is needless for Him to remain or return, as we would not obey the second time better than the first. He not only comes to dwell, but knocks to show what is in the way. I just heard an evangelist tell the following: "A minister was assisting another in meetings. He had never received the spirit which he was seeking and prayed with such power and earnestness as to call the attention of all present, when he suddenly ceased and told the pastor that he almost got him, and it was shown him that one thing more had to be given up; but he would not and left the house a sad, Godforsaken man and went back into the world." I was sent to a successful Holiness minister with a message calling for a sacrifice, but he refused to make it and left his charge and is now working on a farm.

Christ said: "It has been said thou shalt love thy neighbor and hate thine enemy, but I say love your enemies, bless them that curse you, do good to them that hate you and pray for them which despitefully use you and persecute you; that ye may be the children of your Father which is in heaven." This can only be done when our hearts are softened by the spirit of love. John said, "If a man say I love God and hateth his brother, he is a liar; for if he that loveth not his brother whom he hath seen, how can he love God whom he hath not seen. He who loveth God loveth his brother also."

Last summer I heard a paper read on the teachings of Christ, which showed that we must not defend ourselves against the blows of an enemy. In a debate which followed, they said when we saw one beating a weaker person it was our duty to assist him overcome the stronger. But I do not read my Bible so. It is our duty to step between and receive the blow aimed at the other and allow the assailed to escape and plead with the aggressor, as his soul is worth more than our bodies.

A Quaker caught a burglar in his house and instead of turning him over to the officer to be punished, he knelt down with him and prayed and pleaded with him until he was converted and he became a preacher of the gospel. I once assisted in capturing two burglars who broke into a minister's house, who were sent to prison. A year later the minister received a penitent letter from one, a young man, begging him to petition for his release, but I think no notice was taken of it further than to read it from his pulpit.

Pardon coming from the heart is the strongest weapon we can use upon an enemy, but it is one of the scarcest commodities in the market because of the scarcity of the Holy Spirit, the only attribute of love, while the Lord is desirous to bestow Him freely upon us all; without whom we can never come in His presence, nor love Him or our fellow man.

The purpose of this sermon is to show from another standpoint the importance of seeking and obtaining after our conversion the Holy Spirit, without which we cannot, 1st, belong to Christ; 2d, be admitted to His presence; 3d, become a son of God; 4th, become a joint heir and brother of Christ; 5th, escape the great tribulation; 6th, love God nor man; 7th, dwell in the New Jerusalem; 8th, be taught the mysteries of His glorious kingdom; 9th, be translated to God without lasting death; 10th, escape the tribulation at the end of the millennum in which most of those that are saved in this age will fall away. So let us first of all things seek the kingdom and righteousness of God that can only be obtained through His spirit; and with it we shall have peace that surpasses all understanding.

The story of love and hatred may be summed up in few words. When God created Adam he put in him a heart that was all love and incapable of hatred. But his first sin reversed his heart and whole nature, so he became a slave to hatred and incapable of love; so the moral law was given which became his nature and no change was possible until the heart was reversed or changed back. This Christ taught us how to do, and His teachings were followed for 300 years, when the knowledge of obtaining a loving heart was lost and it is impossible to live a loving life without obtaining a loving heart, and that can only be done in the way Christ prescribed, which none of us follow, so you see why we have all failed.

TWENTY-THIRD STEP.

Martin Luther.

" Ye did run well."

No one of this generation knows aught of Luther except what he has read, and no one can write past history but he who has read history. It is told of Alexander the Great that when one came to him with a complaint he would stop one ear so he would have one unbiased to hear the other side of the case. I have read five biographical sketches of Luther, but unfortunately they were all written by friendly hands, so I am not well prepared to write an unbiased history, for a man's friends will tell of his virtues and his enemies his vices. And too, my mother lived and died a Lutheran, and no one would wantonly assail the religion of his mother.

It is not my purpose to give a full history of the man who produced an epoch in the religious world by, in the darkest ages of our history, breaking the galling papal chain that encircled the world and letting Germany go free, and kindling a flame of religious liberty that shot its beams over the earth. I could not tell the half in the space given for a single sermon. No man since the apostolic age has achieved so much for God and the church as Martin Luther.

It is not my purpose to erect a literary monument to the memory of the great man, for the world has repeatedly done that, but to bring to light for the benefit of the Christian public some important items in his history, of which the general public as well as members of his own church are ignorant.

When God has a work to do he raises up a man to do it, and I will briefly show the work that Luther was required to do and how very well he did it. When God first made man he created him with an immortal nature that was incapable of hatred, and had he so remained discord, wars and fighting would have been unknown to the world, for it would have been impossible for lovers to quarrel or immortal men to kill each other. But Adam's first sin changed all of this and turned the friend into a fiend and immortality to death. But what the sin was that did all of this is a subject on which the modern churches are silent. But not so with Luther, for he says, "None of the Fathers of the church before Augustine made mention of original sin, namely, that original sin is to covet lust and desire, which is the root and cause of actual sin." This he correctly confirms in several places in his "Table Talk." In one place he says, "It is to the regenerated a running sore and remains in Christians until they die, and God made marriage for a plaster for the sore." That while God drove Adam out of Paradise for no other crime than contracting a carnal marriage, He has so much been reconciled to carnal men to look with impunity on Adam's sin that He will now take men from the marriage bed to Paradise, or while Adam was driven out for taking one wife, men can now with impunity take in succession from one to four or five. Whitefield called the minister who was living with his fifth wife the much married man. All of this from Luther is a strange mixture of truth and error. His many quotations from the Apostolic Fathers proves him to be ignorant of the writings of most of them, as I believe most of their writings were concealed in his day in the monasteries, where they have since been found. He is in error in saying Augustine was the first who treated on original sin. He died A. D. 430. I have not his writings but do not dispute his statement. But Tertullian, who wrote 250 years before, says, in comparing Adam with Christ, "The last Adam (that is Christ) was entirely unwedded as was even the first Adam before his exile from Paradise." I will not here try to prove the fall as I have not the time, but will leave it for a future sermon, but simply assert that satan the serpent lusted after Eve and humbled her when she tempted Adam.

Ignatius, who lived in the first century and is said to be one of the little children who Christ blessed, said in his address to Satan: "By thy belly or by thine appetite thou wast overcome." Justin, the martyr, who lived in the first part of the second century, says the prince called the serpent fell with a great overthrow because he deceived Eve. Victorinus says, "Who that is the law of God that is filled with the Holy Spirit does not see in his heart that on the same day of the week on which the dragon seduced Eve the angel Gabriel brought the glad tidings to the Virgin Mary and Christ suffered on the same day that Adam fell." Gibbon's "Decline and Fall" says, "The chaste severity of the Fathers in whatever related to the commerce of the two sexes flowed from the same principle; their abhorance of every enjoymnt which might gratify the sexual and degrade the spiritual nature of man. It was their favorite opinion that if Adam had preserved his obedience to the Creator he would have lived forever in a state of virgin purity and some harmless mode might have peopled Paradise with a race of innocent and immortal beings. The use of marriage was permitted only to his fallen posterity as a necessary expedient to continue the human specie and as a restraint, however imperfect, on the natural licentiousness of desire."

So we find that God drove Adam out of Paradise

for contracting a marriage, but permitted him to live still in the world, but hid his face from carnal man but permitted him to still dwell upon the earth, with a promise that he would in the future have the chance of redeeming Paradise, which will be at the close of the millennium. So Moses' law was founded on marriage, which will give them that obeyed it a place on the earth as subjects in Christ's kingdom but not in the heavenly Jerusalem. These will have no part in the first resurrection, which will occur $3\frac{1}{2}$ years before the second or end of the age.

Christ came to bring in a new order of things by teaching that the kingdom and crown belonged to the virgins, and taught that it could only be obtained by suffering. (See Romans 8: 10-17; Hebrews 12: 1-17; I St. Peter 4: 1-4 and 5: 10; and II Tim. 2: 12, and many others). After the church had remained faithful for 300 years they tried to steal a march on the Saviour, which was by teaching virginity without suffering, or their way instead of Christ's, so they neither healed the sore nor applied the plaster and so fell short of both the gospel and the law.

After this long seeming digression I will now return to Luther and see what he did to correct the error. I will not trouble you with a lengthy description of his birth and education. His parents expected to make a lawyer of him and he was educated for it, but in the midst of it his friend and companion was stricken down by his side by a stroke of lightning, which entirely changed his plans and caused him to go into a monastery, where he voluntarily took a vow of celibacy, and where at the age of 20 found the first Bible he had ever heard of, supposing that all the scripture was contained in the prayer book and catechism. A close study of this revealed to him the errors of the church. He was ordained priest in 1507 but did not attack the errors of the church until 1517, when John Tetzel commenced to sell indulgences to raise money to enable the Pope to build St. Peter's Church. Every possible effort was made to compel him to recant but to no purpose. He was filled with that zeal for God and courage that the Holy Spirit only can impart. He was summoned to appear before the Pope's legate and the Emperor at the diet of Worms. His friends tried to persuade him not to go or they would burn him as they had his books recently. He replied that he would go if they set as many devils on him as there were tiles on the roofs of the houses. His ambition was to go and tell the true story of the gospel to the ministers there. The only thing that saved his life was his drawing nearly all of Germany and the most powerful princes on his side. He was before this summoned to meet the Pope's legate at Augsburg, but his effort to get him to recant was futile. He said he would not agree to arrest Luther with 10,000 soldiers, for where the Pope had one on his side Luther had ten. Duke George was his bitterest enemy and his friends advised him to keep from Leipzig, for if Duke George got hold of him he would not get away. He replied, "If I had business at Leipzig I would ride there if it rained Duke Georges for nine days running." Luther was permitted to return from Worms, but was arrested by his friends and taken to a place of concealment where he remained ten months, during which he translated the New Testament into German, which is called the best translation made in any language, for the decree of the diet was that his books should be burned and no one should aid him in any way and he should be arrested and delivered to the Catholic authorities. After the ten month's concealment he again appeared in public in Wurtemburg, but his party was so strong that no one after dared to put the decree of the council in execution.

Luther emerged from his concealment in 1522, and

as far as Luther was concerned the work of the reformation was completed, and it had been accomplished in five years. The papal chain was broken and Germany was free. His publisher called him the third and last Elijah, who is to come just before Christ's second advent and restore to the church the Apostolic faith and practice; but in this of course he was in error.

The next three years of his life is not so glorious, and brings him to the third period of his life, according to Bunsen, his biographer, who divides his life into three periods. First, to 1517, which he calls the preparation, which extends to his 34th year. Second, the period of progressive action to 1525. While he wrote some books during these three years that might have been useful, he used every means in his power to persuade the Nuns, who were under the sacred vow of celibacy, to break their solemn vow. Nine nuns escaped in 1523 and came to him for protection. The next year he threw off his monastic habit, and the next, 1525, at the age of 42 married Catherine Von Bora, who was 20. He had taken the vow of celibacy when he entered the monastery and repeated it when he was ordained priest. God, who cannot lie, cannot look upon any one with any degree of allowance, and if God's word is true a vow of celibacy if sacredly kept is precious with God, who says, "They who shall be accounted worthy to obtain that world and the resurrection from the dead neither marry nor are given in marriage." The ten that went to meet the bridegroom were virgins. One who was asked to the marriage supper said I have married a wife therefore I cannot come. The 144,000 who have part in the first resurrection will be virgins. Clement, Peter's companion, says in his epistle to virgins: "God will give to virgins the kingdom of heaven by reason of his great and noble profession." Even Luther says: "A preacher of the gospel ought above all things first to purify himself before he teaches others. Is he able with a good conscience to remain unmarried let him so remain." He had broken his vow after holding it sacred until he was 42, would it not have been very much better to have continued the fight until the end? He says, "I have yet to learn by experience that any one married for the sole purpose of begetting children to rear in the fear of the Lord."

We have now come to the third period of his life, which was from 1525 to 1546, or 21 years, which the biographer calls the period of stagnation. I was surprised to find a well educated Lutheran minister who could read the testament in seven languages and was ignorant of such a period. The truth is, when he broke his vow God took the Holy Spirit from him and his whole nature changed. Erasmus, the most learned and popular man in Germany, joined the Protestants but could not agree with Luther in his doctrine of election, who held that we were mere machines who could do nothing to gain our salvation, forgetting that God said, "Whosoever will may come." So any one who is not included in God's "whosoever" may be accounted rejected. His friends tried to bring him into Luther's party, as they said if he did he would bring all of Germany with him. Erasmus had made many enemies by defending him and, wrote him friendly letters and called him a great man and said he had learned more from one short page of Luther than from all the large books of Aquinas. He finally wrote a refutation of Luther's election views in favor of Freewill, but in a perfectly friendly manner, making no personal allusions. Luther's friend, Melancthon, promised Erasmus that Luther would answer him with civility and moderation, for Erasmus said in his preface: "You ought not to take this differing in opinion ill because I have allowed you the liberty to differ from Popes,

Cardinals, Universities and Councils of the Church." But like King Saul, the spirit of the Lord and departed from him and an evil spirit had taken possession of him, and as he had broken his promise it was not reasonable that he should verify Melancthon's. His answer was a tissue of personal abuse and falsehood without trying to refute his arguments, and nothing after that was too bad for him to say or do against Erasmus. He calls him the vilest miscreant that ever disgraced the earth, and says that in 1525 (the year the quarrel began) he sent 200 ducats as a present to my wife but I refused to accept them. He was always poor and begged for even his ministerial robes. He calls him accursed wretch and says whenever I pray I pray for a curse upon Erasmus, forgetting God says "bless and curse not."

We will now see the immediate effect of his marriage, for the loss of the spirit would have produced immediate effect. He says he married in haste. His memoir by Alexander Chalmers says he was for some time ashamed of himself and owned that his marriage had made him so despicable that he hoped his humiliation would rejoice the angels and vex the devil. But the devil does not get vexed that way. Melancthon found him so afflicted with what he had done that he wrote some letters of consolation to him. Then he tries to lay the blame on God, who he said commanded it, and wrote to justify himself, but he was not himself satisfied with these reasons. He did not think the step he had taken could be justified on the principles of human prudence, and we find him in other places endeavoring to account for it from supernatural standpoints. The wise men are greatly perplexed. Does any one believe that God, who says in the 15th Psalm, " Who shall stand on thy holy mount? He who sweareth to his own heart and changeth not. He that doeth these things shall never be moved;" will He command one to break his vow? We will let Luther condemn himself. He says in Table Talk that sin brings fear of death. Two years after his marriage he was taken very sick, and recovering a little applied himself to prayer, made a confession of faith, and lamented grievously his unworthiness of martyrdom which he had so often and so arduously desired.

He did not vent all his spite against Erasmus, but vented his spite against the Baptists because they reject infant baptism, which originated in the middle of the 3rd century. Then he turned cannibal and was determined to devour the body and blood of Christ, claiming that the eucharist is the literal body and blood of Christ. Christ had but one literal body and there would not be enough to go around once and what would we do for a carcass for the next meal? The eucharist is not the literal nor spiritual body, but it is figurative, just the same as a hobbyhorse is a figure of a horse. Bunyan in his Holy War tells us how we can eat Christ. He says when Diabolus captured Mansoul (Adam), he made Lord Lusting Lord Mayor, but when Emanuel's army recaptured it they crucified Lusting and then Emanuel took up his abode again in Mansoul, for they that are Christ's have crucified the flesh with its passions and lusts. So when we cleanse our temples Christ who stands at the door and knocks will come in and dwell in us and then we will have eaten His body and blood in a spiritual sense.

With his marriage Luther's spiritual work was done and seemed to be oblivious to all around. The Augsburg diet that formed the creed called the Augsburg confession was held but he did not attend; others had to complete the work. I will now give the whole text: "Ye did run well, what did hinder you that ye should not obey the truth?" Yet Luther saved the church. How? By restoring the law. By the decree of the Council of Nice, A. D. 325.

they rejected the letter of the gospel and tried to still hold to the spirit, which resulted in their losing both the gospel and the law, which I said was founded on marriage. So in restoring marriage to the church Luther restored the law. His sin was not so much in getting married as it was in breaking his vow, so he really sacrificed himself to save the church. So which shall we follow, Luther who takes us back to the law, or Christ who leads to God and his kingdom?

TWENTY-FOURTH STEP.

Adam's Fall.

"In Adam all die."—I Cor. 15: 22.

To the modern church this is an unfathomable mystery; how we could possibly be punishable for a sin committed 6000 years ago, over which we had no possible control, when even the Bible says the child shall not be punished for the sin of the parents; yet it is plain that Adam's sin separated the whole human race from God and subjected them to death as the true penalty. All efforts of modern theologians to give a logical explanation have failed, and some have been honest enough to acknowledge their ignorance and accounted it an unfathomable mystery.

As God is a God of nature, equity and justice, all of his laws must agree thereto; so the penalty must have been the natural result of the sin. So we must (like a physician) first examine the disease to ascertain its cause, which we will find in Genesis, 3rd chapter. The first result was they discovered their nakedness and were ashamed, as Milton says in Paradise Lost:

" But let us now, as in bad plight, devise
What best may, for the present, serve to hide
The parts of each from other that seems most
To shame, obnoxious, and unseemliest seen;
Some tree, whose broad, smooth leaves together sewed,
And girded on our loins, may cover round
Those middle parts; that this new comer, shame,

There sit not and reproach us as unclean."

Nothing but carnal lust could produce this sense of shame, for we see it in the naked savages, who are naked in their childhood but when they come to puberty they, as Milton says:
" And with what skill they had together sewed
To gird their waist, vain covering, if to hide
Their guilt and dreaded shame! O, how unlike
To that first naked glory! Such, of late,
Columbus found the American, to girt
With feather'd cincture. Naked else, and wild
Among the trees on isles and woody shores."

It is self-evident fact that if they had have known lust before the fall they would have discovered their nakedness.

My next witness is Tertullian, who is called the Solomon of the Apostolic Fathers. He says, " Since the last Adam (that is Christ) was entirely unwedded, as was the first Adam before his exile." John Bunyan in his Holy War represents Adam's fall as the taking of Mansoul by Diabolus (the evil one), and says: " He did choose a Lord Mayor himself, and such as contented them to the heart, and such as pleased him wonderous well. The name of the Lord Mayor that was of Diabolus' making was the Lord Lusting, a man that had neither ears nor eyes. All that he did he did naturally, as doth the beast."

Peter says (II Pet. 1: 4) of the saints: " He hath granted unto us his precious and exceeding great promises that through these ye may become partakers of the divine nature, having escaped from the corruption (death) that is in the world by lust." Proving that death comes from lust. And Paul says, " If ye live after the flesh ye shall die." I have produced proof that the mortal disease was carnal lust, which Martin Luther also asserts, but says that marriage is a plaster for the sore, but we well know that it never heals it nor is applied for that purpose, but is to keep the sore running until it runs our life away, and if the plaster gets dead from excessive drawing that it is useless. We are so fearful that the sore will heal that we are apt to apply a green, fresh plaster to start it running again.

The next symptom of the disease is, "God said to the woman, I will greatly multiply thy sorrow and thy conceptions. In sorrow thou shalt bring forth children, and thy desire shall be for thy husband, and he shall rule over thee." This is generally true, but I did read of a case where the wife did the ruling, and another where I thought she ought to. Luther said in his "Table Talk," "I have never learned from experience of one case where a man married for the sole purpose of begetting children to rear to serve the Lord." I wonder if any one else had such an experience? No one dares to deny that excessive childbearing is the natural result of carnal desire. To find the spring we must follow the river upstream. To find the source of lust we must go beyond Adam and Eve. Before God created man he created the innumerable and immortal host of angels and made them all of the male sex for a purpose and gave them power to be both visible and invisible. So they could get offspring without lust, or being perceived had Adam retained his virginity, as in the case of Sarah (Gen. 21: 1-2), and in the case of Mary, who bore a son and still remained a virgin, and I say here that she always remained a virgin, for Joseph was an old widower with a family of grown up children, who are called Christ's brethren, when he espoused her.

These angels differed in strength and position and ability, but were made (like man) in the image of God, and the one called the Serpent had the earth for his dominion and got jealous of Adam for being in possession of the only female of all the beings created in the divine form, so he approached Eve in his visible form not to people the earth with holy beings but to create and feed his own lust and impart it to her for their own selfish gratification and not for God's glory. After this act, which transformed the Serpent into the Devil and Satan (Rev. 12: 9) and kindled the fire of lust in Eve, it was easy for her to do the rest, which entailed lust on the entire human race which eternally separated us from God unless we accept the atonement which Christ came to bring. But that is not a part of this effort for I am only treating the fall.

Christ came to reveal all things connected with the fall, as much of the language in Gensis is figurative on purpose to conceal its meaning until then, for Christ alone was to bring redemption, and to know the disease was necessary to be able to learn its cure. Yet the lascivious (called Christian) church has been more laborious in concealing than revealing the most vital part of Christ's teachings for over 1500 years. The Apostles delivered them to the early Fathers of the church who recorded them, and they have come down to us. The Apostle Andrew said, " Since the first man, Adam, who brought death into the world through the transgression of the tree and been produced from the spotless earth, it was necessary that the son of God should be begotten a perfect man through the spotless virgin, that he should restore eternal life which men had lost through Adam, and should cut off the tree of carnal appetite through the tree of the cross." So you see what tree Adam ate of. Archelaus, an early bishop, says, " For this reason also has he obtained the name of Devil, because he has passed over from the heavenly places and appeared on earth as the disparager of God's commandment." Clement tells us that carnal men are children of the devil. Did not Christ say " Ye are of your father, the devil, and the lusts of your father you will do." If Satan solemnized (?) the first carnal marriage he is the father of it.

Victorinus, an early spiritual writer, says, "Who, then, that is taught in the law of God, who is filled with the Holy Spirit, does not see in his heart that on the same day of the week that on which the dragon seduced Eve the angel Gabriel brought the glad tidings to the Virgin Mary." Justin Martyr says the serpent fell with a great overthrow because he deceived Eve. Ignatius is said to be one of the children that Christ blessed. There are 15 epistles that bear his name. One to St. John, one to Mary, and one to Polycarp. The following is from his address to Satan in his Epistle to the Philippians: "Thou dost set forth thine own fall as an example to the Lord, and dost promise to give Him what is really His own if He would fall down and worship thee; and how didst thou not shudder, O thou spirit most wicked, through thy malevolence than all other wicked spirits to utter such words against the Lord? Through thine appetite (Greek belly) thou wast overcome, and through thy vain glory thou wast brought to dishonor. Thou, O bellial, dragon, apostate, crooked serpent, rebel against God, outcast from Christ, alien from the Holy Ghost, exile from the ranks of angels, reviler of the laws of God, enemy to all that is lawful, who did raise up against the first-formed of men, and didst drive from the command of God those who in no respect injured thee; thou who didst take arms against Job: dost thou say to the Lord, If thou will fall down and worship me? Oh, what audacity! O, what madness! Thou runaway slave, thou incorrigible slave, dost thou rebel against the good Lord? Dost thou say to so great a Lord; the God of all that either thee or the sense can perceive: If Thou wilt fall down and worship me?"

To Adam God said: "In the sweat of thy face

shalt thou eat bread, till thou return unto the ground; for out of it wast thou taken; for dust thou art and unto dust shalt thou return."

No argument is necessary to prove that carnal indulgence will produce all of these results. As God said to Satan, dust shalt thou eat all the days of thy life, so he said to Adam, dust thou art; and so is all of the human family, and Satan has eaten them all up; and Satan and all carnal men go on their belly.

Eden and Paradise are figurative terms and mean God's dwelling place, for He was with Adam before he fell as He is with holy men now. The tree of life is the tree of virginity, which all who obtain Christ's kingdom will have to eat of, for those holy ones who will have part in the first resurrection will not be defiled, for they are virgins, we read in Rev. 14: 4, and these will possess the kingdom, for Clement, Peter's companion and disciple, says: "For God will give to virgins the Kingdom of Heaven by reason of the great and profession." Beausober, an eminent French Protestant writer, says: "It was the prevailing opinion among the earliest Christians that if Adam had not fallen by disobedience he would have lived forever in a state of virgin purity, and that a race of sinless beings would have peopled Paradise produced by some less objectionable means than the union of the first pair of immortals who became mortals." But God never made a mistake. When He made the serpent he knew what he would do, but he told him not to, and the same with Adam. Had there been no devil, no carnal desire, no temptation, there could be no reward for obedience. The dog or horse earns no reward for obeying their master, for that is their nature. Had all earned a kingship there could have been no servants for them to reign over and subsequently no kingdom. So God gave the law of Moses first, so all who obeyed it might have wives and be subjects, while those who obeyed Christ's gospel and became his virgins might be kings and reign over them. Esau typifies the former, who sold his birthright to the kingdom for a morsel of flesh, while Jacob does the latter, who exchanged the flesh for the heirship.

"The time is short," says Paul, "when those who have wives be as if they had none." Zachariah 12: 12-14 says that the families that remain shall mourn every family apart and their wives apart. So you can begin to see what Christ meant when he said unless a man hateth his own wife he cannot be my disciple; and there is neither male nor female in Christ Jesus.

Nearly all of the early Fathers who wrote during the first three centuries, wrote in praise of virginity. Clement wrote two epistles to virgins, filling 12 double column pages. Methodeus' Banquet of the Ten Virgins is grand and complete, filling 50 pages. Tertullian's writings on the subject would fill as many more. What do modern theologians say on the subject? Nothing. Where are the virgins in the modern Protestant church? Echo answers: Where?

The serpent was not the only angel that fell by their lust, for we read in Genesis 6: that when men began to multiply on the earth and daughters were born unto them, that the sons of God (angels) saw that they were fair that they took them wives of all that they chose, and their children were giants, whom the Lord sent the flood to destroy. II Peter 2: 4 and Jude 6: speaks of them, and a number of the Apostolic Fathers, from which I quote Laclantius: "When, therefore, men had begun to increase, God in his foresight, lest the devil, to whom from the beginning He had given power over the earth, should by his subtlety either corrupt or destroy men, as he had done at first, sent angels for the protection and improvement of the human race; and inasmuch as he had given these a freewill He enjoined them above all things not to defile themselves with contamination from the earth and thus lose the dignity of their heavenly nature. He plainly prohibited them from that which He knew that they would do, that they might entertain no hope of pardon. Therefore, while they abode among men, that most deceitful ruler of the earth by his very association gradually enticed them to vice and polluted them by intercourse with women. Then not being admitted into heaven on account of their sins into which they had plunged themselves, they fell to the earth. Thus from angels the devil made them to become his satellites and attendants. But they who were born from them, because they were neither angels nor men, but being a kind of mixed nature, were not admitted into hell, as their fathers were not into heaven. Thus there came to be two kinds of demons; one of heaven and the other of earth. The latter are the wicked spirits, the author of all the evil that is done, and the devil is their prince." Their bodies were destroyed in the flood, but their immortal spirits compass the earth seeking bodies to dwell in. When they possess our bodies they are the author of every evil thought, desire or dream. The best way is to starve them out is by fastings, as Christ did during his 40 days' temptation, and we need not wonder the demons wanted the stones turned into bread, as they enjoy our feasts with us, and abstinence from worldly pleasure, which is necessary if we approach near to God. (See Exodus 19: 14-15, I Cor. 7:5, I Sam. 21:4, and Rev. 14:4.)

If God banished the holy angels from heaven and would not permit them to see his face for no other sin than taking a wife; how about us, guilty of the same fault? Is God such a respecter of persons that he will condemn to eternal fire (for that will be their final end) for one crime, one being, and set another on his throne to judge him who is guilty of the same, and that unrepented of? Know ye not that ye shall judge angels. The Holy Spirit if followed will always lead to virginity. The children of this world are wiser than the children of light.

I consider the Mormons the farthest from Christ of any church that claims the name of Christ, and they teach that Satan seduced Eve and she tempted Adam, and repeat the play in their temple worship. One taking Adam's and another Eve's and another Satan's and another God's part. Thus admitting that Adam lost Paradise by a carnal marriage. The query is: If Adam lost Paradise by taking one wife, can they retain it by taking two or more. They say we are not punishable for Adam's sin. I should think we are punishable for our sin if we commit the same, for what was sin against God 6000 years ago is sin to-day. I believe that Ann Lee, the founder of the Shakers, was led by the spirit of God to embrace virginity, but afterward the devil came to her as an angel of light and made her believe she was Christ, and led her and all of her followers astray. I was under a similar influence for three days, and the tempter told me I could make all believe I was Christ and bring the world to my feet. The virginity of the Catholic priests is not acceptable to God and does not lead to the kingdom, but I cannot explain here. I have shown you how Paradise was lost, and leave you to guess how it can be regained.

TWENTY-FIFTH STEP.

Virginity.

"Having, therefore, these promises, beloved, let us cleanse ourselves from all defilement of flesh and spirit, perfecting holiness in the fear of God."—II Cor. 7:1, R. V.

The promises are in the previous verses and are, "Come ye out from among them and be ye separate, saith the Lord, and touch no unclean thing; and I will receive you and will be to you a father and ye shall be to me sons and daughters, saith the Lord Almighty."

No part of the Christian religion is so much ignored by the Protestant churches as the subject of virginity, and none of their clergymen can recommend it without condemning their own lives, yet it is one of the doors that we must surely pass through before we can be admitted into Christ's presence or have part in the first resurrection, as you will read in Rev. 14: 1-5. Verse four says, "These are they which were not defiled with women, for they are virgins. These are they that follow the Lamb whithersoever He goeth. These were purchased from among men to be the first fruits unto God and the Lamb. And in their mouth was found no lie. They are without blemish."

This happy company is limited to 144,000, yet it is the privilege of each of you to be one of them. Virginity alone does not admit into the kingdom of Christ, for ten in the parable came to the door but five only were admitted. The Roman Catholics make a boast of their priests, monks and nuns, but I fear they will mostly be found with the foolish virgins, for they refuse to follow Christ everywhere and trample the most vital of his teachings, and even now they are departing from that, for a prominent priest recently startled the world by urging his virgins to marry, and said there were sixty virgins in his church that he would like to see brought to the altar; and other priests have taken up the cue. Yet in teaching virginity I have been accused of teaching Romanism. Do Christ and the Apostles teach virginity? Jesus said, " The sons of this world marry, and are given in marriage; but they that are accounted worthy to attain to that world and the (first) resurrection from the dead, neither marry nor are given in marriage; for neither can they die any more, for they are equal unto the angels and are sons of God being sons of the resurrection." To the feast of the kingdom Christ said of those that bought land and oxen, " Have me excused." They could come but preferred to stay away; but one said, " I have married me a wife, therefore I cannot come to your virgins' banquet." In Matt. 19: 10-12, offers virginity to all able to receive it, and says, " Ask and ye shall receive, for he that asketh receiveth." Paul says, " Art thou loose from a wife? Seek not a wife. But this I say, brethren, the time is shortened that henceforth both those that have wives may be as though they had none. She that is unmarried is careful for the things of the Lord that she may be holy both in body and spirit."

I have given ample proof that to any one that is willing to believe the Bible that Christ and the Apostles taught virginity. But they permitted marriage to those who could not or would not accept it, but at an unfathomable loss. God permitted marriage under the old law but barred them from his presence. Priests were washed and kept from their families eight days before they could minister before the Lord. No woman was admitted in the temple. The congregation had to separate themselves three days before God would come to give them the law. How is it with modern ministers? Did the Apostolic Fathers teach virginity? There are eight volumes of their writings, containing over 5,000 double column pages, that have been suppressed for 1500 years because they taught virginity. They can now be had at Charles Scribner's Sons for $20, which is about half what mine cost. I think enough is written on the subject in them to fill one of the volumes of 600 pages. They treat the subject fully. One article fills 50 pages, and nearly every writer has written in its praise and none against it. An attempt to quote them would be to exceed my present alloted space and I have quoted some under other heads.

What will we gain by virginity? We will become a son of God, a joint heir to the kingdom and crown with Christ and reign eternally with Him; be subjected to no more temptations and have eternal rest with God and never taste death.

What will we lose or gain by rejecting it? We will have to die; will have to suffer in the great tribulation, and if we are saved we will be banished from Christ's presence and the Holy City; be subjected to another temptation at the close of the millennium, when most of them who have been subjects will be lost.

TWENTY-SIXTH STEP.

The Fish Story.

"As Jonah was three days and three nights in the whale's belly; so shall the son of man be three days and three nights in the heart of the earth."—Matt. 12: 40.

Infidels have taken great delight in flinging Jonah's fish story at people who claim to believe the Bible. In short it is about the only argument they have to prove the untruthfulness of the Bible.

The Irishman called Jonah the "whale 'ater."

"Well, Sambo, what did the minister preach about?"

"'Bout de mighty big miracle."

"What was it about?"

"He told 'bout the 12 'postles eating 5000 loaves of bread and 5000 fishes."

"What was the miracle, as there seems to be plenty for them?"

"Why, they ate it all and did not burst."

Robert Ingersoll asked a Professor if the Bible said that Jonah swallowed the whale would he believe it? He said he would; why not? Martin Luther tells of a man who swallowed a horse and wagon, and claimed to furnish the proof, and no one would think of questioning Martin's statement, and after a man had practiced on a few horses and wagons it would not be difficult for him to swallow a whale. Of course none but a wizard could do it, and Martin was a firm believer in witchcraft, and tells many stories just as unnatural. One was of a wife who died and was buried, came back to her husband and lived with him several years and had several children, but she suddenly disappeared leaving her robes behind because he swore. He pointed to the children for proof.

I had an intemperate neighbor who went into a saloon and told the loungers to look down his throat as there was something in it; which they did. Don't you see anything, he asked. They said, no. You ought to, he replied, for I have swallowed two farms.

Avowed infidels have not been alone in denying the truth of Jonah's whale story. Beecher's Plymouth successor gained much unpopular notoriety by calling the book of Jonah a novel.

We will now consider some of the reasons that its opponents give for rejecting the book. First, that the whale lives on insects and has not a throat large enough to swallow a whole apple. Answer—The word whale does not occur in the book of Jonah, and the word in the text is an error of the translator, and whale is not in the Greek. The account reads, God prepared a great fish, and if God could make so large a fish to swallow a bug He could make a smaller one to swallow a man. Sharks and crocodiles can swallow a large fish, and I have seen a snake swallow a toad larger than itself.

Second, a man could not live in a fish's belly. Answer—Neither could you live in a furnace of fire nor in a caldron of burning oil; but men have. Could not God keep Jonah alive three days in the fish's belly as well as he could you nine months in your mother's, unless you happened to be a seven months' issue or an incubator baby.

Third, the Jews were a despised race and their preaching would not be accepted in a foreign country. If a Spaniard landed in New York and went up Broadway preachings, "Hear ye! Hear ye! In 40 days this city shall be overthrown." Do you think the Mayor and city officials would exchange their broadcloth for sackcloth and proclaim a fast for man and beast? Not a bit of it. But the preacher would land in a lunatic asylum before he had got many blocks. Answer—It may be true, but a prophet is not without honor save in his own country. The Ninevites were heathens and worshipers of the god Dragon, who they believed came out of the sea and was half man and half fish. God never made a mistake, and he did not mean to send Jonah on a fool's errand, as He did Jeremiah and others who he sent to preach to Jerusalem, and probably would if he had gone directly to Ninevah; but God knew that he would not and prepared accordingly. So Jonah started for Tarshish to run away from the Lord, which resulted in the conversion of the ship's crew, which was a good start for a missionary. Next he converted the fish—into a submarine packet; and finally reached Ninevah; not as a Jew, but as a representative of their god Dragon, who came from a fish out of the sea, and they could not deny him without denying their god. The result was the whole city (probably as large as New York) repented in sackcloth and ashes and fasted and turned from their evil ways and cried mightily unto God, who heard them and spared their city.

After Jonah had gained their confidence as a representative of Dragon he had no trouble to point them to the true God. Now can you see the wisdom of God in using those means to bring that great city to repentence.

This was doubtless the most successful missionary journey of the world's history, and the only case where the missionary got angry " even unto death " at the success of his preaching.

Ninevah repented and was saved for a time, probably during that generation, but it went back to idolatry, which caused it eternal destruction, for the want of another Jonah. It requires no great argument to prove that the Ninevites were sinners, for the king said, "Let them turn every one from their evil ways, and from the violence that is in their hands." The question is, was Nineveh any more corrupt than New York is to-day, which has not the excuse of ignorance that the former had, that there were more than six score thousand persons who cannot discern between their right hand and their left hand. Has not Tammany extorted from the people whenever she ruled since the days of the Tweed ring, and is not the present Mayor with his ice trust refusing the tormented poor a drop of cold water to cool their parched tongues? I see their dragon or fish god swallowing the whole city with its rum greed and lust. It would take an army of Parkhursts to save the city. The one they turned into a Jonah and swallowed him up but failed to turn themselves into Ninevites and repent at his preaching. So the city will surely have to be overthrown, for God says, "There was a great earthquake such as was not since men were upon the earth so mightily and the cities of the nations fell." So this does not apply to New York alone, for "the soul that sinneth it shall die" applies to all, and these dreadful days are just before us, so it behooves every one to repent.

TWENTY-SEVENTH STEP.

Free Methodist Holiness.

Except our righteousness exceed the righteousness of the Scribes and Pharisees, ye shall in no wise enter into the Kingdom or Heaven.—Matt. 5: 20.

Soon after Luther had broken the papal chain England fell in line. These things occurred during the reign of Henry the Eighth, who wrote a book against some of Luther's teachings, for which the Pope honored him with the title of "Defender of the Faith." Soon after he asked the Pope to annul his marriage that he could marry Anna Belone; but the Pope was so slow about it and he could not wait, so he broke allegiance with the Pope and established the Episcopal Church, after the form of the Catholic, only put himself at its head instead of the Pope. But the church dropped some of the gross errors of the parent and very many very good men have been enrolled among its members; among which was John Wesley, who was a close student of the Bible and taught holiness, and with Whitefield was instrumental in many thousand conversions, which he offered to the mother church, but she refused to receive them, so he was obliged to organize the Methodist Episcopal Church, which has done a very great work for the Lord, and counts her members by the millions; but he never left the parent church and died in it.

In the world's history no church has gained wealth and popularity without losing its deep piety, and the Methodist was no exception; so like Jeshurun (the upright one), they "waxed fat and wicked." Some years ago some of their ministers tried to bring them back to their former faith and teachings, but succeeded only in getting expelled from the church, so they organized the Free Methodist Church, which corrected many errors of the mother church. I have enjoyed attending many of their meetings and give them the credit of holding more truth than any of the old churches; but their ministers admit that they are not living up to the standard of 20 years ago. They teach perfection, and many claim to have received the Holy Spirit, or "a clean heart" as they call it, and live without sinning.

I attended one of their meetings recently when the pastor was absent and an old man who had been presiding elder or chairman 12 years took his place. I had never met him before. He took for his subject the 7th of Romans, which says: "The law is spiritual; but I am carnal, sold under sin, for what I do I know not; for not what I would that do I practice; but what I hate that I do, for to will is present with me; but to do that which is good is not, for the good which I would I do not; but the evil which I would not that I do. I find then the law, that to me who would do good evil is present. O wretched man that I am! Who shall deliver me out of the body of this death."

The Free Methodist hold that after a man has received the spirit he will no longer sin, and as Paul received Him by the laying on of Ananias' hands (Acts, 9: 17) at least 20 years before he wrote the above, it is in their way and must be got out. So the preacher said that Paul was not giving his experience in this 7th of Romans, but that of impenitent sinners, and it applied to him before his conversion but not then, and that sinners hated sin. Yet Paul said that before his conversion he was a strict Pharisee, and as touching the law, blameless;

and the Word says, "The wicked delight to do evil, they do it with both hands."

The Free Methodist like all other modern holiness teachers are, either ignorantly or otherwise, trying to steal a march upon the Lord, or to get a crown without paying the price; and if Paul meant sinners and not himself when he said "I and me," he lied over 40 times in the last 20 verses of this chapter, which is putting them in very thick. But he meant just what he said, and his experience is the same as any man's who will obtain the kingdom.

As I have repeatedly stated, conversion does not relieve us from temptation, but removes love for sin, and the temptation for sin is stronger than the hatred of it and forces us to do what we would not, and like Paul, the things we hate them we do, because Satan rules our bodies. Neither does the Spirit help us or relieve us of Satan's power, but will lead us to a scourging or chastening, which will cause bodily suffering which will drive Satan from us for ever and remove all desire for sin and make us sons of God and perfect.

Paul knew what was between him and perfection, but a Roman law stood between him and its acceptance that it was very hard for him to get over, as he tells us in Phil. 3: 8-16, "That I may know him and the power of his resurrection and the power of his suffering; becoming conformed unto his death, if by any means I may attain unto the resurrection of the dead. Not that I have already obtained, or am already made perfect; but I press on, if so be that I may apprehend that for which I was apprehended by Christ."

You see here he was seeking for some peculiar suffering that was to make him perfect and enable him to attain to the first resurrection, for "Blessed and Holy is he that hath part in the first resurrection, for on such the second death hath no power."

But he after this obtained his coveted treasure, for in Col. 1: 24-29, he says, "Now I rejoice in my sufferings for your sake, and fill up on my part that which is lacking of the afflictions of Christ in my flesh, for his body's sake, which is the church." He also says in Galatians: "I bear branded in my body the marks of Jesus, and, I have been crucified with Christ, yet I live and yet no longer I, but Christ liveth in me," and, "They that are of Christ have crucified the flesh with its passions and lusts."

We know that Paul wrote Romans, I Corinthians and Philippians before he identified himself with Christ by bearing his cross, and Hebrews, Galatians and Colossians, and probably II Corinthians, Ephesians, Thessalonians, Titus and Timothy after. He says in Rom. 8: 17, "We are sons of God and joint heirs with Christ if so be that we have suffered together with him," and to Timothy, "If ye suffer ye shall reign with Him," and in Hebrews, 12: "If ye do not suffer ye are bastards and not sons." So if your righteousness does not exceed the righteousness of the Free Methodist and all others of like faith, you cannot enter into the kingdom of God.

www.ingramcontent.com/pod-product-compliance
Lightning Source LLC
Chambersburg PA
CBHW020916230426
43666CB00008B/1468